# THE EXCEPTIONAL LIFE OF AN ORDINARY MAN

A JOURNEY TO BECOME THE MASTER OF GLOBAL BONDS & CURRENCY MARKETS WITH A STOP IN HOLLYWOOD

TIMOTHY JOSEPH MICHAEL O'GRADY

# CONTENTS

*Preface* ............................................................................. v

1. The Journey Begins ........................................................ 1
2. Work Ethic .................................................................... 11
3. Eisenhower ................................................................... 17
4. Lorraine Phillips ........................................................... 25
5. Until The 12th Of Never ............................................... 33
6. A Later Start in Life Helped My Success ....................... 41
7. Pushing The Envelope ................................................... 53
8. Starting Over Again ...................................................... 68
9. Two Guys In Hartford .................................................. 73
10. A Fortune Teller ............................................................ 80
11. Building Fixed Income Research ................................... 93
12. Picking Fixed Income Managers .................................... 108
13. The O'Grady Family Moves To Weston ........................ 114
14. Pictures Up ................................................................... 120
15. Taking The Message To The People .............................. 126
16. Western Asset Management Company .......................... 134
17. Director ........................................................................ 144
18. Hollywood .................................................................... 164
19. Thank You And Goodbye! ............................................ 178
20. FX Concepts ................................................................. 184
21. Prague Six ..................................................................... 195
22. ROW Asset Management .............................................. 202
23. Camino de Santiago "Way Of St. James" ...................... 215
24. Sin-Free ........................................................................ 222
25. ROWAM: Building A Business ..................................... 238
26. The Next Step ............................................................... 242
    Appendix ...................................................................... 244

*About the Author* ............................................................. 251
*Acknowledgments* ............................................................ 253

Copyright 2024 by Timothy Joseph Michael O'Grady

All rights reserved

No part of this book may be used or reproduced in any manner without written permission from the author.

Cover design: 99 Designs.com

Book Formatter: Robert Harrison

Published in the USA by: Timothy Joseph Michael O'Grady

ISBN:

# PREFACE

Writing a memoir was one of the most challenging endeavors of my life. It was not a decision I made lightly; it was prostate cancer that ultimately nudged me toward retirement at age seventy-six in 2021. During recovery period, I enrolled in a four-day writing course titled 'Writing a Memoir', with a simple directive to write about something I knew intimately—myself. Little did I realize that delving into my own story would provide an exploration into uncharted territory. I discovered that I did not truly know myself as well as I had thought. I decided to focus my memoir on my journey toward becoming one of the Masters of the Global Fixed Income Universe. Over the years, I had the privilege of collaborating with numerous investment experts, many of whom have since become familiar faces on television and the internet. These experiences form the backbone of my memoir and offer insights into the intricacies of the financial world as well as the personal and professional growth that accompanied my endeavors.

As a first-generation college student, I carried my parents' aspirations, a dream they harbored even before I entered this world. They had a clear vision for me: to become a teacher. Growing up, I excelled at West Main Street Grammar School, consistently making the honor roll and delivering the eighth-grade salutatory speech. Despite the challenges of balancing school with my parents' work schedules, I managed to maintain perfect attendance from third through eighth grade. Both parents worked, illness was not an option in our household.

When I attended Southern Connecticut State College (SCSC) in New Haven Connecticut, I initially aimed at pursuing a teaching degree, but my academic journey took an unexpected turn. In 1967, I graduated as SCSC's first Economics Major, earning a Bachelor of Arts degree in Economics. However, my academic path was not without hurdles. I started off on probation the first year and a half and faced academic challenges along the way. It was during this time that I crossed paths with Lorraine Phillips, a freshman at SCSC. Meeting her marked a pivotal moment in my life, and our bond has remained steadfast throughout the years—we recently celebrated our 55th wedding anniversary. Her unwavering love and support have been instrumental in shaping my journey. Despite the initial setbacks, I persevered and eventually made significant improvements in my grades, consistently earning a spot on the dean's list. Ultimately, this turnaround opened the door to graduate school for me.

I did not tell my parents until my senior year in college that I was not going to be a teacher. They were very disappointed. However, as I reflect on my career path, I realize that although I did not become a teacher in the traditional sense, I spent the majority of my professional life mentoring and educating some of the most talented individuals in every role I took. In many ways, my memoir is as much their story as it is mine, as it highlights the profound impact they had on me and the invaluable lessons I learned from them.

1

## THE JOURNEY BEGINS

Growing up in Milford, Connecticut, nothing in my childhood hinted at the business career I would later embark on, a career focused on navigating the intricate world of fixed income securities (bonds), foreign currencies, and their derivatives.

Nor could I have envisioned my part-time Hollywood background-acting gig that started in 2005 at age 60 after my wife Lorraine and I moved to California in 1999. I was on the big screen for about eight minutes on the movie Iron Man #2 (2010) in the Senate scene which ended with me hugging Robert Downey Jr. Each movie shot is done several times from different angles. Robert and I got to be screen friends.

My journey in finance commenced at a Connecticut bank before leading me to positions at progressively larger organizations. I transitioned to a prominent New York mutual life insurance company and a leading east coast pension consulting firm. However, it was at the age of fifty-four that I made a pivotal move to join a major west coast bond manager. During my tenure there, the firm became the world's largest fixed income manager. My next assignment was building a fixed income program for world's largest privately owned foreign currency manager.

In 2012, I embarked on a venture to establish a fixed income investment firm in Prague, the Czech Republic. Despite my efforts, the endeavor did not materialize. Subsequently, I joined my son Ryan O'Grady's hedge fund ROW Asset Management (ROWAM) in Newport Beach, California. During my tenure at ROWAM, firm assets under management (AUM) expanded from $13 million to more than $2 billion. My journey with ROWAM concluded with my retirement in December 2021 at the age of 76.

Communication challenges me. My soft voice is attributed to years of heavy smoking and a tendency to mumble, yet I excelled in front of a microphone and an audience, delivering at least two speeches annually on fixed income and currency investments across various venues in the USA, Toronto, Canada, and London, England. Additionally, I authored several investment 'white papers'. I worked hard and was non-confrontational to ensure that my ideas were effectively conveyed, albeit sometimes taking longer than anticipated.

Starting on O'Grady genealogy studies later in life, I pursued the goal of obtaining dual USA/Irish citizenship and acquiring an Irish EU passport. The establishment of the European Union (EU) in 2000 presented an opportunity for seamless travel across European countries with an Irish EU passport. This document would streamline my currency research travels throughout Europe, granting easier access to twenty-seven Euro countries' customs checkpoints where I held up my passport and walked through.

Both of my grandfathers were immigrants who married daughters of immigrants. In the early 1900s, immigrants like my maternal grandfather, Andrew Michael Bekech, along with an older sister embarked on a daunting voyage to Bremen, Germany, to catch the steamship Breslau to NYC when he was 15 years old arriving Feb. 24, 1906. They had to sell their family cow to finance their passage, which symbolized real wealth in Slovakia (then part of the Austro-Hungarian Empire). Upon arrival in New York City, customs officials anglicized and spelled out Grandpa's last name as Bekech. Bridgeport, Connecticut, served as a destination for many immigrants from the Austro-Hungarian Empire, particularly those of Slovak and Hungarian descent.

*became BEKECH*

On the other side of my family, the O'Gradys trace their roots back to Athenry, County Galway, County Clare, Ireland. They joined a wave of immigrants who arrived in the United States during the mid-19th century, just after the start of Irish famine (1845–1852). The O'Grady family shares the immigration narrative with other well-known families, such as the Kennedys (1849), Obamas (1850), Bidens (1855) and Reagans (1857), who all arrived within a relatively short span of eight years.

In 1852, my great uncle, Thomas O'Grady, and sister Catherine were forced to leave the O'Grady farm and mill lease in Athenry, County Galway when the lease was sold. They began on a challenging journey across Ireland by train to Dublin, then by boat to Liverpool, England. From there, they boarded a three-masted schooner, a sailing ship named Barque Atalia bound for New York. The voyage across the Atlantic relied on wind and weather conditions and could take anywhere from a month to three months. Sadly, many of these sailing ships were infamously referred to as 'coffin ships' due to the high mortality rates of passengers, ranging from 10% to 20%. The Barque Atalia Manifest listed Thomas as a Miller; Catherine was noted as a house maid. (Catherine was seventeen years old in 1852; it may have been safer for her to be twenty years when traveling.)

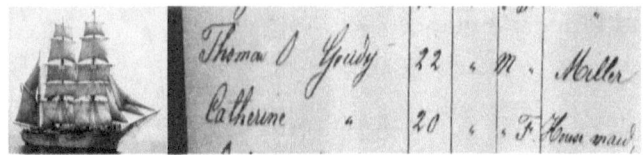

Thomas' success as a builder in Boston suggests that he had the means to sponsor members of the O'Grady family members like my grandfather, Peter O'Grady. Additionally, Mary O'Grady, Thomas O'Grady's daughter, rose to prominence as Superior Mary Immaculata within the Catholic Church on the East Coast. She played a significant role in sponsoring Irish families.

In Irish families where a member pursued a religious vocation, it was not uncommon for the Catholic Church to provide financial assistance, known as 'Catholic Celery', to aid in immigration expenses. Superior Mary Immaculata's influence and connections within the Catholic Church facilitated the immigration of several Irish families. It is also reasonable to conclude that Superior Mary Immaculata suggested Milford using the resources of the Milford Catholic Nunnery to help assist the O'Grady family move from Boston in 1917–1919.

The 1920 U.S. Census for Milford Connecticut reveals insights into my family's immigration history and residence. Notably, the address, 123 West Main Street, was close to our long-time family home at 100 Plains Road. The Census shows my paternal grandfather, Peter O'Grady, immigrated to the USA at the age of 13 in

1889. My maternal family lived nearby Stratford and Bridgeport, fostering regular interactions between the two sides of my family as I grew up.

My parents, Thomas (Tim) O'Grady and Mary Ann Bekech, married twice due to a dispute between Eastern Catholic priests, who were permitted to marry, and Roman Catholic priests, who were bound to celibacy. The first ceremony was in my mother's church in Bridgeport, the second at my father's church in Milford before mom got pregnant. To ensure the legitimacy of their marriage and Catholic upbringing of their future children, my parents decided to cover their bases by remarrying in Saint Mary's Catholic Church.

For nearly a decade, my parents grappled with infertility before doctors finally diagnosed mom with a medical issue. Despite the challenge, they both worked and saved to buy an acre of land at 100 Plains Road, Milford, CT, where they built their dream home in 1939. Mom's medical issue was resolved, and after her recovery I arrived in 1945, followed by my brother Tom two years later. Although my parents were overjoyed to have us, my brother and I both displayed symptoms of hyperactive ADHD, and we had our fair share of disagreements and fights.

Growing up in the picturesque town of Milford was a stroke of luck. Nestled along the shores of Long Island Sound, it sits between two of the Connecticut's largest cities, Bridgeport and New Haven. Water has always been a central theme in my life, as is evident by our vacation home in Vermont and our residences in California, all of which are situated on or near water.

Milford's rich history dates back to its settlement in 1636, making it the sixth oldest city in Connecticut. The Town Green, New England's longest, serves as a gathering place for community events and adds to the town's charm. With the longest shoreline on the Long Island Sound among all Connecticut communities, Milford offers endless opportunities for beach walks and the stunning Sound's blue waters.

Just a few miles offshore from Milford lies Charles Island, linked to Silver Sands State Park by a natural tidal sandbar. Charles Island is steeped in legends of the notorious pirate Captain Kidd who visited Milford in 1699. Local lore suggests that Captain Kidd may have buried a portion of his treasure on the Island. However, the existence of the treasure and its exact location remain a mystery, buried beneath the sands of time.

Growing up, my parents bore the weight of significant responsibilities within their families. As the eldest, my mother had to help raise five brothers and a sister while managing household tasks, as my grandmother struggled with housekeeping. Meanwhile, my father, the eldest of six, faced additional burdens due to his alcoholic father and his spendthrift mother.

My brother Tom and I, along with our cousins, often heard stories of the O'Grady boys walking along the New Haven Railroad tracks in Milford, picking up coal that fell off the coal cars to heat the family apartment. With limited financial resources, food and other necessities were often scarce, let alone funds for medical care, especially considering my father's asthma and the ill health of his brothers, Uncle Peter and Uncle Jack. Despite these adversities, my dad and his brothers James (Nug), Joe, and Jack emerged as some of the best athletes Milford produced. Uncle Joe, in particular, achieved remarkable success as an All-American football player during his freshman year and again his senior year (after World War II) at American International College (AIC). He later became a coach and then athletic director at AIC, leaving a lasting impact on the institution.

Aunt Anne blazed the trail becoming Milford's first cheerleader and leaving her mark on the basketball court. She played a pivotal role in three consecutive undefeated teams at Milford High. In recognition of their outstanding athletic achievements and contributions to the local sports community, I am actively involved in petitioning for the inclusion of my father, Uncle Nug, Uncle Joe, Uncle Jack, and Aunt Anne into the Milford Sports Hall of Fame.

Fibbers Bar and Restaurant, owned by Uncle Nug and his wife Ann, became a cornerstone of Milford's social scene, akin to the iconic bar featured on the TV show Cheers. Both Dad and Mom contributed to its success, with Dad working part-time nights as a bartender and Mom serving as a waitress on busy weekends. The O'Grady family was well known in town.

Thanksgiving held a special place in our family's heart, serving as a rare occasion for all my aunts uncles and cousins to gather. Our home at 100 Plains Road became the central hub of these gatherings, where Mom, Dad, and the rest of the family diligently prepared meals throughout the day.

During the mid-1950s, a cherished tradition was born: the O'Grady Thanksgiving Football Games. The family was divided into two teams: the Tiger Sharks led by Cousin David Murcko and me and the Black Hawks led by Tom and Uncle Bob Bekech. Rain or shine, our spirited matches unfolded, with rain adding an extra layer of excitement to the game. We would dash into the house to change our clothes quickly, hoping to avoid any relatives catching us, all while the festivities continued in the basement below.

The two pictures from November 1951 capture an O'Grady

family Thanksgiving dinner in our basement at 100 Plains Road. It is our own rendition of Norman Rockwell's 'Freedom from Want' painting. The picture on the right captures me as I am watching dad carve up the turkey. On the left side, I am sneaking in from the right side.

In the mid-1990s, my brother Tom and I decided to revive the tradition of the Thanksgiving O'Grady Games, but this time in Weston, Connecticut, at our home on Singing Oaks Drive. Before its subdivision into three-acre lots, Singing Oaks had once been a campground. We purchased the model home. Remnants of the old campground—including a basketball court—lingered, waiting for me to clean it up for use in basketball and roller hockey. I made hockey goals for our roller hockey game. The Thanksgiving tradition continued even after our move to California, albeit with a slight shift in focus. Touch football and bowling became the new highlights of our holiday gathering in the 2000s, proving to be equally enjoyable alternatives.

One fall day, a decision was made to convert our half-acre vegetable garden on Plains Road into a baseball field. Dad decided Tommy and I were ready to start playing baseball. Tom and I were happy because we hated weeding, watering, and gathering horse manure for fertilizer for our garden from the local riding trail across the street.

From the moment we could lift a bat, Dad began coaching us in the art of batting left-handed, despite our natural inclination to bat right-handed. He emphasized the strategic advantage of batting left-handed, as it positioned us a step and a half closer to first base. More importantly, Dad instilled in us a love for team sports by teaching us to play with determination, take calculated risks, and relish the recognition that comes with athletic achievement. With Dad as our coach, we couldn't have asked for a better mentor on and off the field.

Dad's dedication to our baseball development extended beyond merely converting our backyard into a makeshift field. He meticulously constructed a baseball backstop in the right back corner of our horizontal property, strategically placing it so that left-handed hitters like us had ample space to drive the ball. Under Dad's guidance, we learned to hit the opposite field, forcing the third baseman or shortstop to make long throws across the diamond to first base. Despite working the 7:00 a.m.–3:00 p.m. shift in Bridgeport and then coming home to start dinner, Dad always made time to practice with us after work. We often continued until dusk if he did not have to work at Fibbers Bar & Restaurant.

Tom and I shared a competitive spirit and constantly pushed each other to excel. Despite being younger, Tom was a superior player, and leveling the playing field for both of us became a nightly challenge for Dad. His efforts didn't just enhance our skills; they also expanded our circle of friends, as our yard became a hub for neighborhood kids, all drawn to the desire to play baseball. Our neighborhood playground was such a comfort growing up that I would create the same neighborhood play area in my backyard in Watertown, CT 25 years later.

I enjoyed playing hockey at the Lily Pond, located west down Plains Road. Although Milford lacked a hockey team, the pond attracted players from neighboring towns. Dad, though not a hockey player himself, ensured I had the necessary gear, even opting for figure skates over hockey skates for added ankle protection and maneuverability. Dad's meticulous attention to detail did not go unnoticed; he always sought to give me every advantage possible.

While I enjoyed success playing hockey, my experience with Little League baseball presented a different challenge. I was on the team for two years but I was not a starter. We never lost and ran the score up against every team we played. Dad worked and Mom did not drive, so if I wanted to play baseball, I had to call my teammates' parents for a ride to and from games. None of my classmates, neighbors, or friends were on my team, so it was painful to call the parents of kids I did not know well to get a ride to sit on the bench. As I got older, I rode my bike to the games and told my parents I was riding to someone's house for a ride. My parents never attended my baseball games. I made a promise that as soon as I could, I would earn enough money to buy my own car and never ask anyone ever for a ride. From that moment on, nothing motivated me more than the desire to carve out my own path and never rely on anyone for assistance.

# 2

## WORK ETHIC

In my family, work ethic was ingrained from a young age. Both my parents worked full-time jobs, with additional part-time work on the side. On top of that, they tended to our half-acre vegetable garden, which provided produce for our dinner table. During the fall, my mom, her mother, and her sister Frances put up vegetables for winter use.

Although I never matched my parents' level of work, I had my share of responsibilities, particularly in tending to our yard as I grew older. Our expansive lawn, which also served as a baseball field, demanded a Briggs & Stratton gasoline-powered lawn mower—a rarity in our neighborhood. Initially, I relished the task of mowing the lawn. But as I matured and our circumstances changed, it became more of a chore, especially with my commitments to playing baseball on the high school field. Whenever possible, I tried to pass off the duty to my brother.

Each summer, my dad's two-week vacation coincided with the annual factory shut down for maintenance, a common tradition in factory towns. These weeks became opportunities for household projects. One year, he painted our entire house alone, using only a ladder and a paintbrush. Another summer, he replaced the screens on our porch with my brother Tom and me lending a hand. As a reward, we got to sleep out on the porch during warm summer nights—a rare treat since none of our neighbors had a screened porch.

During a brutal snowstorm between December 1960 and February 1961, I faced the daunting task of delivering The Bridgeport Post to 120 customers on my paper route. With help from Teddy Mikita, I abandoned my Robin Hood bike and walked through the deep snow. Despite the challenging conditions, I made sure to deliver each newspaper directly to the door, knowing that my customers relied on their daily news and wouldn't want to go out in the storm. Some neighbors called my parents to let them know that I was still delivering papers and had not frozen. Upon returning home, my family appreciated my dedication, but they suggested it was time for me to explore other opportunities beyond newspaper delivery, since I was exhausted and cold.

You could always make money by picking vegetables at 25 cents an hour at Kuchma's Truck Farm on Saturdays 8:00 a.m.–12:00 p.m. My dad made me stop because I was falling asleep at the dinner table. (For reference. a gallon of regular gas was twenty-five cents; I could buy four gallons. Today in California, four gallons of gas would cost $22.)

On my sixteenth birthday on June 7, 1961, my dad surprised me with a life-changing gift: my State of Connecticut Working Papers and a full-time summer job at W T Grant's store at the new Connecticut Post Shopping Center. Dad's connections ensured my employment, and although getting to work and back was my responsibility, I saved every penny except the bus fare from Carvel's Ice Cream store. I also paid a neighbor, Junior Booth, a cook at WT Grant, for a ride home at night. To this day, the Connecticut Post remains the largest mall in the state.

At seventeen, I enrolled in driver's training in the summer of

1962. My driving instructor, Mr. Donohoe, was a teacher at Jonathan Law High School and a familiar face from my days at Milford High. Mr. Donohoe, a hockey referee himself, was aware of my involvement at the Lily Pond and extended an unexpected invitation one day after a driving lesson: to assist him in refereeing a game at Madison Square Garden in NYC. I declined despite feeling honored. Eager to reciprocate, I invited Mr. Donohoe to a hockey game at the Lily Pond where his expertise left everyone in awe.

My dad helped me transition into adulthood by arranging for me to take my driver's test and surprising me with a 1958 Chevy Bel Air, 2-door coupe. He had purchased the car using the money I had saved in my Milford Savings Bank account. As a devout Chevy enthusiast, he ensured that I became a Chevy owner like him, a gesture that caught me off guard. I had previously expressed the desire for more independence and the ability to work longer hours with my own car.

Owning my car was a transformative moment that elevated my social status and encouraged my involvement in high school activities for the first time. In 1962, Michael Connors and I were the only two kids in high school who had their own cars and weren't reliant on parents' vehicles.

Dad arranged for me to work at the Stuart L. White Company, a Milford-based Fire Protection Engineers firm. I held a part-time position throughout high school and college and transitioned to full-time during vacations and summers. Patty Fogg, Uncle Nug's eldest daughter, served as the secretary for the owners. This job covered my expenses and financed my college tuition and apartment rentals during my academic pursuits. By working up to twenty-four hours during school and forty-four hours during summers and vacations, I achieved my goal of independence by the age of seventeen.

During my time at Stuart L. White's, I had to handle dry ice which has a bone-chilling surface temperature of -109.3 degrees

Fahrenheit. This hazardous task required special gloves to protect against the extreme cold. Dry ice under pressure becomes liquid $CO_2$ and is subsequently pumped into a fire extinguisher. Despite precautions handling dry ice, I have no fingerprints.

In June 1980, Colonial Bank & Trust promoted me to Treasurer, a Senior Officer position. When asked to provide fingerprints to the Federal Reserve, multiple attempts by Waterbury Police resulted only in smudges. I became an anomaly in the banking world, without any fingerprints on file with federal authorities. Later in life, this situation posed challenges for security agencies and notaries and rendered biometric securities features, such as fingerprint locks on cell phones, ineffective for me.

The Bullard Machine Company in Bridgeport, CT, where my Grandpa Bekech worked most of his life, was a significant factor in my parents' emphasis on college. Grandpa Bekech secured positions for his sons, and his son-in-law at Bullard's Foundry, except for Uncle George. Uncle George held an impressive thirty-five-year tenure as an executive in Bullard's Head Office adjacent to the foundry.

When Stuart L. White assigned me to Bullard's in the 1960s, two of my uncles still worked there: Uncle George in the main office and Uncle John Murcko in the foundry. When I was assigned to check fire extinguishers in the Foundry, a large building with blast furnaces, I would see Uncle John.

Entering the foundry was daunting; it resembled an airplane hangar filled with heat, smoke, and noise. Limited visibility due to thick foundry smoke made inspecting the fire extinguishers on the ceiling cranes and along the building walls challenging. Working with the cranes required climbing a ladder to signal the crane operator to bring the crane over so that I could inspect the fire extinguisher on the crane. Once done, the ceiling crane operator took me to the next ceiling crane operator to check an extinguisher. I traveled from crane to crane as I traversed the top of the foundry.

Despite my apprehension, the crane operators were understanding as I made my way across the ceiling.

Amidst the chaotic activity on the foundry floor, I kept asking foundry floor workers where John Murcko was located. Their vague directions pointed toward the center of the bustling workspace. Cloaked in the haze of smoke and noise, Uncle John was a distant figure, diligently working away on a form while puffing on his Lucky Strike cigarettes. He was surprised I found him. He knew I was coming but not at that time of day. The noise made talking difficult. His dedication to his craft was a testament to the hard-working spirit that permeated the foundry.

The foundry floor workers were incredibly accommodating and helped me locate the empty $CO_2$ fire extinguishers that needed refilling. Amidst the challenging environment of the foundry, they shared a clever trick for chilling beers after a hard day's work: simply place the nozzle of a 20-pound fire extinguisher over a can of beer, give it a little squirt, and wait for the magic to happen. It was a refreshing way to unwind with ice-cold beers straight from the foundry.

My first experience of paid vacation at Stuart L. White Company came five years later in August 1967, and it was nothing short of unforgettable. Alongside my friends Dave Pesapane and Ed McCarthy, I embarked on a journey to Chicago to witness the NFL Champion Green Bay Packers take on the College Football All-Stars at Soldier Field. Dave's college roommate Bob Hyland happened to be the Packers top draft choice, adding an extra layer of excitement for me being a Packer fan. (The 34th Annual Allstar Football Game (August 1967) is on YouTube. I have watched it but did not see myself.)

After the game, Bob Hyland arranged for us to visit the College All-Star locker room where we had the incredible opportunity to meet and talk to the legendary Packers Head Football Coach Vince Lombardi. As we exited the locker room with Coach Lombardi, I found myself unexpectedly handed programs and footballs to sign, as if I were one of the College All-Stars. In a moment of camaraderie and shared enthusiasm, I proudly signed memorabilia alongside these revered athletes, forever etching my name in the annals of football history.

On November 14, 1997, I became a Green Bay Packer 'owner-shareholder', a part of the unique ownership structure of the only corporate-owned football team in the National Football League (see Certificate in Appendix). Additionally, on January 26, 1997, I attended Superbowl XXXII at the Louisiana Superdome where the Packers emerged victorious against the New England Patriots. My seat was just two rows from the ceiling of the Superdome positioned perfectly on the endzone line where Brett Favre executed his memorable touchdown run. I could not resist the opportunity to walk up the two rows and touch the dome ceiling.

3

# EISENHOWER

For me, Milford was country living at its best until the presidency of Dwight D. Eisenhower in 1952 reshaped the landscape with the ambitious vision of a modern highway system.

General Eisenhower, the Allied Commander in Europe during World War II, faced logistical challenges moving troops and equipment across the European theater. Eisenhower recognized the strategic importance of efficient transportation networks and initiated plans for a major east coast highway even before his formal election to the presidency.

US-Interstate-95 was a monumental project that spanned the length of the eastern seaboard, connecting the Canadian border to the sunny shores of Miami, Florida. In Connecticut, the highway traced its path along the scenic Long Island Sound, threading through the heart of the state's population centers.

US-I 95 was designed with more exits than usual to ease traffic congestion on the historic Boston Post Road. Dating back to 1763, this road served as the main communication and commerce route between New York and Boston, part of the original thirteen colonies' north-south network. As the first postal route between New York and Boston, it was part of the Kings Highway commissioned by King Charles of England and stretched from Charleston, South Carolina to Boston, Massachusetts. George Washington and his troops traveled on this highway during the fight for independence. Washington even rested in Milford for a night.

Plains Road, a quaint two-lane paved thoroughfare etched into the oldest Milford maps, was thrust into the spotlight as the designated exit #36 of the Interstate Highway System. The northbound exit emerged just three homes away from our house, and so did a Mobil Gas Station nearby, which supplanted two neighboring homes in the process.

Eisenhower's 1956 reelection campaign highlighted three major achievements from his first term: resolving the Korean War, promoting the 'atoms for peace' initiative, implementing strategic Cold War policies such as the 'New Look Policy' and the Domino theory, and advancing the ambitious Interstate Highway System.

Repurposing material from vacant farm barns slated for demolition to build docks, rafts, and clubhouses was common practice among friends in the area. In the summer of 1956, this inspired me to construct a rustic 'shack' in our backyard beyond our baseball complex. It was to be bigger than any structure built so far. To my surprise, my dad lending me his tools for the project caused a significant change in our relationship as I could only use them when he was around.

Riding my bike to Harrison & Gould's store in downtown Milford to buy cement for the four-post foundation became a routine task. I'd buy a bag, balance it on the handlebars of my bike and ride home. It never felt like work to me. Each night my dad inspected my progress on the construction, offering guidance and asking questions. With his support, we repurposed a large old picture window and a weathered screen door, transforming them into my cherished shack. I believe he took as much pride in the shack as I did.

Then in July 1958, the shack had to come down. My father received an unexpected bill amounting to $100 levied as a tax on the existence of the separate 'out building'. Real estate assessments, conducted via aerial photography, revealed our shack tucked away in our backyard, triggering the unwelcome financial burden. I had put our shack way back in our yard, beyond the baseball field so that you could not see it from our house, the road, or anywhere in the neighborhood.

I saw the picture. My dad fought the issue but was told to take down the building or pay an annual $100 tax. I have one picture of the shack taken with one of those cameras that you clicked a button and pulled out the lens—a very precious commodity to the O'Grady's and very rarely used. I guess the shack qualified as something unusual because dad took a picture.

Plains Road, nestled between Interstate 95 and The Boston Post Road, quickly became a target for rezoning to industrial, which resulted in potential tax hikes. My parents recruited me to aid in their opposition campaign. Positioned atop the new bridge over I-95, I meticulously logged the license plates of 18-wheel trucks exiting at southbound exit #36 onto Plains Road, a violation of rural road regulations.

Despite the risk of being caught, I recorded license plates with each passing truck, but the results were dishearteningly ineffective. Complaints about violators seemed to vanish into bureaucratic oblivion, leaving the neighborhood to contend with the encroaching industrial presence.

Weeks later, the once-sleepy quarter-mile stretch of Plains Road leading to the Boston Post Road was expanded to accommodate the influx of truck traffic. The proximity of Secondi Brothers Truck Stop on the Boston Post Road exacerbated the situation, as the incessant hum of turnpike traffic became an unwelcome addition to our doorstep.

It gets worse. Beard Sand & Gravel owned and worked a sizable gravel pit behind our one-acre property. As soon as Dad bought the property in 1939, he had the foresight to plant evergreen trees along our boundaries to shield us from the noise and to maintain our privacy. For years, this natural barrier effectively buffered the sounds of machinery and trucks as they worked the gravel pit.

Beard's property bordered ours, and one day they boldly plowed a crude gravel road on their adjacent property, mere inches from our property line. This makeshift thoroughfare served as a direct conduit for their dump trucks, facilitating expedient access between their gravel pit to Plains Road. Incensed by this flagrant disregard for residential boundaries, Dad wasted no time lodging a formal complaint to the City of Milford.

Thankfully, the City intervened by erecting a wooden blockade to seal off the unauthorized road, a belated attempt to stem the tide of industrial encroachment. However, the damage had already been done. Our once tranquil homesite had been irreversibly altered. The rural charm that my parents found in 1939 and that Tom and I found in the 1950s was eroded by the march of industrial progress.

In the mid-1950s, amidst industrial expansion, Milford faced another challenge: militarization due to Cold War tensions. The U.S. Government sought land on Eels Hill Road and Rock Lane for a Nike Ajax Missile launch site. Milford had twelve of these formidable 34-foot-long missiles at their base of operations to protect the area from airborne threats.

In October 1955, President Eisenhower visited Connecticut to inspect hurricane and flood damage affecting U.S. military suppliers: Sikorsky Helicopter, Perkin Elmer, and Milford's Nike Ajax Missile site. Eager to see one up close, President Eisenhower requested to see a missile raised into a vertical launch position.

During the Cuban Missile Crisis in October 1962, the Milford Nike Site was placed on high alert, known as Battle Stations. For two tense weeks, personnel remained on duty around the clock in preparation for nuclear confrontation. The looming threat of annihilation cast a cloud of uncertainty over everyone.

The rapid transition of Milford from a quaint town to a bustling city seemed to occur almost overnight, mirroring the broader demographic shifts of the Baby Boomer era. Milford changed from a town to a city government in 1959 because the population jumped from 5,000 in 1940 to 42,000 in 1960. The peak at 51,000 in 1970 signaled the dawn of a new era for the community.

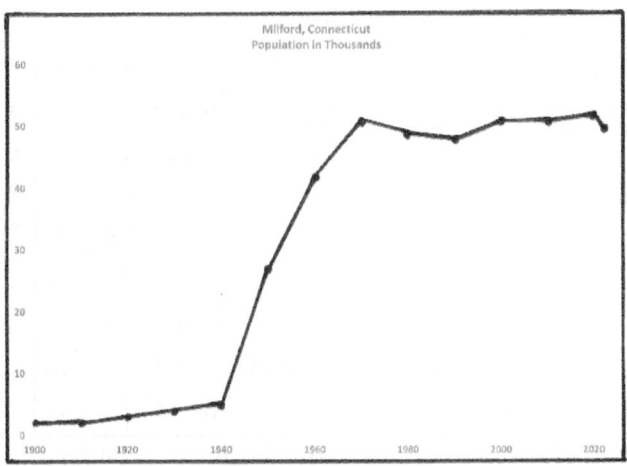

The educational landscape underwent seismic shifts to accommodate the burgeoning student population. The opening of Jonathan Law High School in 1961 provided much-needed relief by splitting the student body between the new institution and the existing Milford High School.

I attended West Main Street grammar school with forty-four kids, the same kids for nine years, split evenly with boys and girls. Less than half of our eighth-grade class was in college prep. The introduction of vocational programs underscored the evolving priorities of education, with trades education becoming as valued as traditional academic pursuits.

I eventually made new friends. John Stankevich, Andy Margonis, Jim DeVack, John Kricker, Stan Kavan, and Tony Alessie were all from the Devon area of Milford where Jonathan Law High School was being built. At the end of my sophomore year, I had the option to continue at Milford High in the center of Milford or to attend the new Jonathan Law High School in Devon. My parents were surprised at my decision to attend Jonathan Law High. Despite the longer commute, which required me to walk up Plains Road each day to Beaver Brook Road to catch the Jonathan Law bus—a walk longer than to Milford High—I wanted a fresh start.

I auditioned for *Rebel without a Cause* at Jonathan Law and landed a non-speaking part as Tire Chain Timmy. It was directed by Mrs. Lee Hart, an English teacher at Jonathan Law, and the wife of former Presidential candidate Gary Hart. Gary Hart was attending Yale Divinity School at that time. Initially, I did not realize the commitment required for rehearsals and had to leave the play due to work obligations. Mrs. Hart was disappointed, which surprised me given my minor role. Nobody replaced me. It was not until 2007 that I had my acting debut on the TV show *The Closer*.

In 1984, Mrs. Lee Hart came back to Jonathan Law High School for a rally and received a picture of her that had appeared in the 1963 yearbook. "This will be on the walls of the White House," she said. The picture Mrs. Hart received can be seen on next page (without the writing). Mrs. Hart is seated in the front, the last person on the right. She did not sign my yearbook.

I received a letter dated February 27, 1963, from Southern Connecticut State College. In it, Robert C. Porter, Director of Admissions, notified me of my acceptance. Before June 1, 1963, I had to pay $50 for my first semester tuition and $38.25 in fees. The fees included a $25 Activity fee, $6 Insurance fee, $2.25 Physical Education Fees, and a $5 Student-Personnel Fee. According to an enclosed form, I also needed a physical exam. The physician himself should return the medical form to Dr. Dorothy Granoff, College Physician, Health Office.

When I arrived at the Southern Connecticut State College campus for the first time, I was unprepared. I lacked a college tour experience and had not even tried to locate the campus before sending in my paperwork. Parking was a challenge since only spots for teachers were available. I ran late and hastily parked and rushed to my meeting with Robert Porter. Despite the delay, our interaction was brief as I confirmed my decision. After registering, I headed home before I got a parking ticket. My parents were thrilled. It was not until my graduation in June 1967 that my parents visited the campus for the first and only time.

At graduation from Jonathan Law, I was honored with the History award for achieving the highest grades in the subject. I also received the Daughters of the American Revolution Certificate award, which provided $100 toward my initial costs at Southern Connecticut. I was recommended for both awards by my engaging history teachers Joseph Carberry and Robert Cox whose classes were interesting and enjoyable.

# 4

# LORRAINE PHILLIPS

In June 1963, as I celebrated my 18th birthday, I was required to register with The U.S. Selective Service System and receive my draft card. Despite the ongoing army draft, the lack of any significant wars during that time meant that the draft card's true significance lied in its role as a rite of passage, serving as evidence of reaching adulthood. I could legally drink in New York State. I had to wait until I was twenty-one to drink in Connecticut.

With my first-year college schedule in hand in 1963, balancing studies with my part-time job at the Stuart L. White Company was crucial for financial stability. I earned extra by doing piece work like hydrostatic testing of fire extinguishers and scuba tanks inside the shop, which added $1.00 per hour to my pay. I managed to cover expenses with $40 weekly earnings by maintaining a routine of breakfast at home, lunch at school, and a late dinner at home. Three dollars filled the gas tank.

The incoming first-year class at Southern had to exceed 1200 students, a testament to the institution's growth. Yet statistics revealed the sobering reality that a third of first-year college students drop out before their sophomore year, with three-quarters of those being first-generation college students. I knew what was in front of me.

I was different during my first week in college than when I started high school. I had grown up during the summer and decided to try out for the Southern Freshman Football team as a right guard. I had never played football, never practiced, and had never even worn a helmet. I was assigned jersey number 36. Guard numbers are between 60 and 69, so I knew there were at least ten players ahead of me on the freshman team.

The loud noise through the football helmet's ear holes was startling as I practiced alongside first-year students returning from the Army. Their superior skill and athleticism humbled me and revealed the team's competitiveness. Despite my excitement, my dad's disapproval and reminder to prioritize studies prompted me to quit the team the next day. Looking back, it was the correct decision.

As I navigated my first year of college, I found myself immersed in a curriculum filled with required subjects, many of which I struggled to grasp their practical applicability in my future. As I trudged through these classes, doubts began creeping in about my chosen path of becoming a teacher.

Despite my passion for history and my knack of retaining details, the thought of teaching the same subject for years left me feeling uneasy. I feared the prospect of becoming stagnant, trapped in a repetitive cycle that did not resonate with my ever-evolving personality.

Gradually, I began to question whether teaching was truly the right fit for me. This realization was disconcerting, especially considering it was a long-nurtured childhood dream. It forced me to confront the misalignment between my career aspirations and my evolving sense of self.

As a Gemini, I have always been aware of the inherent duality within me represented by the twins. On one side, I've harbored a deep-seated drive for innovation, coupled with a love for creative pursuits and storytelling. However, alongside these traits, I have struggled with indecisiveness and inconsistency, common characteristics of my astrological sign. I will admit, there have been times when my stubbornness has surfaced, particularly when dealing with persistent ducks determined to turn my boat dock into their personal restroom.

As a right-brained Gemini, I have acknowledged my inclination toward visual and intuitive thinking, favoring creativity over structure. I naturally gravitated toward companions who excelled in logical and analytical thinking, skills that I lacked but valued greatly.

As I had three years to figure out my future, I kept my thoughts to myself and I navigated through college life. It was during this time that I forged friendships with Frank Milone and Thomas Peckingham who shared many of my mandatory first-year classes. Frank introduced me to their friends Bob Hauser and Lou DaRienzo who both attended nearby colleges. Our bond formed in 1963 and has stood the test of time. Frank and Tom served as groomsmen at my wedding. In 2018, Frank, Tom, Bob, Lou, and their wives joined Lorraine and me in Milford, Connecticut to commemorate our 50$^{th}$ wedding anniversary.

The first semester of my sophomore year proved to be a challenge. I struggled to summon the same level of enthusiasm for my studies, and consequently, my grades suffered. As the semester drew to a close, I found myself placed on probation—a stark wake-up call that prompted me to reassess my priorities.

In the second semester, my improved grades signaled a turnaround. During this time, I crossed paths with Lorraine Phillips, a classmate in my botany class. Fate had us sitting next to each other, thanks to Chester Bosworth's alphabetized seating arrangement—O'Grady followed by Phillips. Lorraine worked in the Southern Admissions Office on a scholarship and she possessed an innate charm that made conversations effortless, even from our very first encounter.

Linda Steele, a high school friend from Jonathan Law High School, and fellow art student with Lorraine brought Lorraine by my locker to say hello. This gave us more time to talk. Eventually, I started walking through the main building, checking my locker more frequently. If I were smart, I could have asked Linda to get me Lorraine's class schedule, since they were both art majors.

I screwed up on the botany final by moving the microscope glass slides to get a better picture. Lorraine was behind me in the class, so me screwing around reduced her botany final grade average to 89, a B; one of her few Bs in four years of college.

As the semester progressed, my feelings for Lorraine evolved beyond friendship. At Southern, Mike Katz was a notable figure—a star football player, weightlifter, and amateur bodybuilder. Post-college he played football for the New York Jets and was a professional bodybuilder. Being into weights myself, I often saw him in the Southern weight room.

One day, one of Mike's minions—yes, he had people—approached Southern Admissions Office, where Lorraine worked part-time through four years of college, to convey Mike's interest in a date. Lorraine promptly declined the offer. When she mentioned this encounter to me, I was really upset.

While I was lifting weights later on, I spotted Mike and decided to confront the situation head-on. I went right over to him and said, "I am dating Lorraine, have been for a while, and we do not need you!" Mike paused his workout and stared at me but—to my surprise—he did not utter a word. Eventually, he resumed lifting, and from then on, he did not again ask Lorraine out or have anyone else intervene on his behalf.

Lorraine's academic achievements were remarkable and she maintained excellent grades throughout as an honor student all four years. Her leadership skills were evident as she served as the 1968

Senior Class President and was a member of the student senate. Additionally, she held prestigious positions such as President of Kappa Delta Epsilon, a membership in Omicron Psi Lambda, both honorary societies. Lorraine made "Who's Who in American Universities and Colleges."

Our time together at Southern was limited and conflicting class and work commitments kept us apart. One evening I went to her place for an early dinner at her off-campus rental on Ellsworth Avenue. Lorraine made spaghetti after which she took out her guitar and played some songs. I really liked that she kept her hair in pig tails and still I like it today when she does that. We talked for a long time until it was late, but I had to leave to get to work.

Our first date was a blend of friendly competition and getting to know each other. Lorraine and I went bowling, followed by a round of pool at Milford Ten Pin. To my surprise, she thoroughly trashed me at both games. Determined to redeem myself, I suggested we play ping pong in the basement at my home at 100 Plains Road. Unfortunately, my skills did not fare any better, and Lorraine emerged victorious once again.

Our ping pong game was interrupted by my parents' unexpected return home. I never had a girl in the house when my parents were away, and my parents knew my girlfriend Linda, which was not Lorraine. I came up from the basement and said, "Hi, This is a friend from Southern—Lorraine, she is from New Jersey." My parents were very polite and said 'hello' but were more concerned whether I fed our beagle, Patrick, than what I was doing or not doing in the basement. Before Lorraine and I played ping pong, I had cooked some eggs. Lorraine thought I was cooking for her, but the eggs were for Patrick who liked them sunny side up. Lorraine was surprised at that. She was having soup or eating Kraft Dinner every day. In 1965, Kraft macaroni and cheese was five boxes for $1 and Lorraine got three meals from one box. Cracker Jacks—with a prize in the box—were a nickel a box.

In the summer of 1965, I played softball nights and on Sundays, I would represent the Center Parkade Package Store in the West Haven Soft Ball League. Over the next years, I played for the Hillside Inn Bar in Branford, and later for the Three Brothers Restaurant in New Haven. Hillside Inn had uniforms for our team, not just a shirt. The Three Brothers had jackets made for us. Lorraine designed the jacket, the lettering, and the beer mug symbol on the jacket.

By the start of my junior year, I made a pivotal decision to change my major to economics from history. This decision was influenced by the emergence of economics as a new discipline at Southern, spearheaded by Professor Jere W. Clark. I embraced the transition from a teacher's program to liberal arts despite uncertainties about the availability of enough economics courses to graduate with an economics major. What mattered most was that I finally felt comfortable with a path forward. Amidst these academic shifts, my relationship with Lorraine remained constant.

As my junior year progressed, my academic performance continued to improve. In my first semester junior year I got a 3.0 average, narrowly missing the 3.2 mark required for the dean's list. I was really upset, and I let the professor know. I considered myself on the dean's list and told my parents. In my second semester junior year, I took the next step toward my independence by renting an apartment at the Elmhurst on 367 Elm Street in New Haven with Frank Milone from Southern and Bob Hauser. Pictured are the three roommates—me, Bob Hauser, and Frank Milone. This picture was taken a few years later at my Ivy Circle apartment in West Haven.

In my second semester of my junior year, my academic performance soared to a 3.4 average with straight As in economics and history. Lorraine's invaluable assistance in refining my writing and typing skills for college economic papers played a significant role. Her help greatly contributed to my acceptance into graduate school in 1967.

Once I got my life focused in the right direction, I knew I had one and a half years to get my grades up for graduate school. My buddy Frank Milone worked at the Yale Law School Library in New Haven and recommended that I use it to study at night after work.
Frank would walk both Lorraine and me into the library as if we were law students. We quickly became regulars and eventually just walked in ourselves. We studied on Thursday and Friday nights, staying until midnight. Smoking was allowed, which seemed to help us concentrate. Afterward, I would drive Lorraine home before her curfew. These sessions enhanced our academic pursuits and strengthened our bond as we navigated higher education together.

Juggling a 24-hour work week, attending college, and managing the responsibilities of living in a downtown New Haven apartment made achieving a 3.4 average a daunting goal. The challenges were compounded by nearby temptations (the Elmhurst Apartment building was located next to a liquor store and faced Ruby's Bar across the street). Bart Giamatti, Yale President (1978-1986), later followed us a customer at Ruby's, eventually attracting Yale students.

For the summer of 1966, Lorraine had the incredible opportunity to travel to Turkey on a scholarship through the School for International Training in Vermont. Unsure of what to do, I turned to my closest friends, Frank and Louie, for help. They graciously agreed to drive Lorraine to Vermont so that she could start her training. She had to learn enough Turkish to communicate. Although I did not join them on the trip, I stayed connected with Lorraine through her letters throughout the summer from Vermont and later in Turkey. Frank Milone wrote to Lorraine in Turkey about our baseball and drinking exploits.

In the backdrop of Milford, my days fell into a repetitive rhythm of work, interspersed with softball games and nights spent at local bars. I found myself grappling with a sense of aimlessness and disconnection. During this time of emptiness, I made impulsive decisions, like getting a tattoo in Newport Beach, Rhode Island, without fully understanding the consequences.

Toward the end of August, Lorraine called me from New Jersey. Worried about the possibility of her moving on without me, I reached out and arranged to meet her. As I traveled down to New Jersey, I felt a mix of anticipation and longing to reconnect. Despite the absence of her trademark pigtails, our reunion felt natural and effortless and as though she had never left. I told her I was going to rent a home at Laurel Beach in Milford to live in during my senior year. I simply did not want to live at home. My parents agreed.

5

## UNTIL THE 12TH OF NEVER

In the summer of 1967, as I transitioned from college to graduate school, I sold my 1962 Chevy convertible, my second car, and bought a junk car, a 1955 two-door Chevy, previously used by Southern New England Telephone Company. The trade-in netted me $600, which helped finance my graduate studies at the University of Rhode Island (URI). I secured a graduate school loan from Second New Haven Bank to cover additional expenses such as tuition, books, and meals.

I junked the 1955 Chevy in Rhode Island on my last day at school at the end of May, 1968. With no brakes, driving became increasingly difficult, especially during the final week of school. I received $50 for it but I had to drive it to the junk yard lot which was no easy feat. URI classmate Brian McGuinness from Stamford, Ct drove me back home to Milford.

Before classes began, Lorraine and I explored potential rental options near the URI campus in Kingston, Rhode Island. Although renting a beach home in Green Hill Beach, Wakefield, seemed impractical for the school year, the allure of the nearby Atlantic Ocean captivated me. I settled on a beach home on Hilltop Avenue and paid a month's rent in advance, using a bonus from the Stuart L. White Company. The owners were impressed that a company I left gave me a bonus, plus they liked Lorraine.

A month later, on a Saturday morning, the family returned to check up on Lorraine and me. As I was studying at the kitchen table, the doorbell rang, and I greeted them alone. They were surprised it was just me there, which suggested that they would be hesitant to rent to a single man and preferred a couple instead. Determined to prove my reliability, I diligently maintained the cleanliness and orderliness of the home to reassure them.

It took some time, but I eventually found a suitable roommate in Bill, a local high school teacher and URI master's graduate who was working on his doctorate. With Bill's understanding of my weekend absence and his willingness to share household responsibilities, we established a living relationship that benefited both of us. Bill often had his girlfriend join him on weekends.

At URI, my classes were small, often consisting of just a few students, including myself, Sid Feld, Brian McGuiness, and Tom O'Keefe. Throughout my time at URI, Lorraine held on to some letters I sent to her revealing my loneliness, financial concerns, and academic pressure. I had to learn economics material for the first time in order to supplement what I was being taught in class. Some of the economics material was entirely new to me, and I had to work hard to grasp it. I was determined to get all As. I stocked up on cigarettes and coffee and studied. Despite the challenges, I eagerly anticipated weekends when I could reunite with Lorraine and my college friends—Frank, Tom, Louie, and Bob.

In December 1967, despite lacking the extra funds for an engagement ring, Lorraine and I had already scoped out a ring at Sears in case I proposed. When I did, Lorraine said 'yes', eager to get the engagement ring that day, even though it was late. As a Gemini known for changing my mind, Lorraine had planned ahead. Whenever she asked about our wedding date, I often teased her by replying "on the twelfth," invoking the phrase "The Twelfth of Never." Little did I know that Lorraine, a devoted Johnny Mathias fan, would find special significance in his song *Until the Twelfth of Never*, which would become our wedding song.

On the afternoon of Tuesday, January 23, 1968, I prepared to head home after my last fall semester exam at URI despite the ominous snowstorm sweeping across Southern New England. I had packed my car the night before, and I braced myself for the treacherous journey, fueled by the desire to see Lorraine. As I set out on Route I-95, the snowfall intensified, accompanied by gusty winds the buffeted my car. During the winter chaos, news of the USS Pueblo's capture by North Koreans blasted over the radio.

As I navigated the snowy highway, I found refuge behind an 18-wheeler and trailed it all the way from New London to Milford. The journey was eerily quiet, with no vehicles in sight. I maintained the same pace with the truck, breezing through three toll booths without a second thought. Anticipation mounted as I neared Lorraine's residence at 5 Laurel Court, Woodmont, Connecticut, only to find a note on her front door redirecting me to my parents' house due to inclement weather. Disappointed but undeterred, I made my way to my parents' home, eager to reunite with Lorraine, albeit sans her trademark pigtails.

In the summer of 1968, I decided not to return to graduate school at the University of Rhode Island (URI) to take the two classes required to finish my economics master's degree. Throughout my year at graduate school in Rhode Island (September 1967 through May 1968) I commuted home each Friday to see Lorraine on the weekend and returned on Sunday. However, as much as I cherished those weekends together, I could not bear the thought of continuing this routine for another year.

I did not want to leave Lorraine Phillips. I missed her when she spent the summer of 1966 in Turkey on a scholarship. The next summer, her junior year, I only saw her for a few hours on Sunday because Lorraine worked and lived at the Cherry Lawn School, in Darien. These moments were all too brief, and each goodbye was tough.

Returning to the University of Rhode Island did not seem financially feasible for me. I only had two required graduate-level economic courses left to complete my master's program. Fortunately, those courses were available at the University of Bridgeport (UB). With my course work completed, I had the flexibility to spend the next three and half years writing my master's thesis at home. This decision provided me with the opportunity to devote more time building a life with Lorraine while continuing my academic goals in a more manageable setting.

In August I reached out to my advisor at the University of Rhode Island (URI) at his home to inform him of my decision not to return. I also asked for approval on two courses from the University of Bridgeport Connecticut (UB) that aligned my program. Understandably, my advisor was upset as my slot in the graduate program could have gone to another student. Unbeknown to me, URI had even planned for me to teach a freshman economics class. After some negotiation and persuasion, my adviser approved the UB courses. I completed these courses over the next two semesters at UB and successfully transferred them back to URI.

Since I met Lorraine in 1964, I often found myself humming a song by Kenny Rogers that would not be written until 1981: *Through the Years*. Its lyrics perfectly captured the meaning of our relationship. Through the years, our bond only grew stronger, and the song became a beautiful reminder of the love and support we shared.

Receiving that letter from Second New Haven National Bank in early September 1968 was a stark confirmation of my new reality—I was no longer a full-time student. Faced with the responsibility of repaying my graduate school loan, I made a conscious decision not to burden my parents with financial strain. Instead, I took the first job offered to me: financial analysis/marketing at Winchester Western Repeating Arms in New Haven, Ct.

It was quite surprising when Winchester Western Repeating Arms offered me the position, considering my lack of qualifications required for the position, whether it be in accounting, marketing, or military experience. Nevertheless, I was hired on the spot and started work the next day. I mentioned to the Winchester Human Resources department that I was to be married on Saturday, December 7 and they graciously approved a week off starting December 9.

On Saturday December 7, 1968, Lorraine Phillips and I exchanged vows in Ridgefield Park, New Jersey at Lorraine's family church, Saint Mary the Virgin Episcopal Church. Lorraine looked radiant in a wedding dress she had crafted herself; she would proudly wear the same dress 50 years later at our golden anniversary.

After attending the wedding rehearsal and celebratory dinner, everyone in the wedding party except for Lorraine—the bride to be—headed off to Howard Johnson's to join everyone else from Connecticut. We were all looking forward to relaxing with a few cold drinks. However, the inconvenience of having to constantly go down the hall and get ice prompted someone to come up with a mischievous idea. Before we knew it, the ice machine was unplugged and brought into Tommy and my room.

About an hour later, there was a sudden knock on the door. When I opened it, I was greeted by two imposing figures-members of the New Jersey State Police. They informed us that they had been called to investigate a missing ice machine and intended to walk around the complex to search for it. If we saw it, we should please inform them. After they went up the stairs to the next floor, we unplugged the ice machine, left some beer in it, and placed it back where it belonged.

My Uncle Van and my father showed up the next morning at

Howard Johnson's to pick up Tommy (my best man) and me for a ride to the church. My Uncle Van backed into one of the fences when turning around to leave. I guessed my uncle and my dad had a few cold ones the night before also. Our wedding date was the last week of 1968 before hotel rates and airplane rates increased for the Caribbean 'winter holidays'.

During a break from our wedding festivities to dress for our honeymoon, Lorraine and I opened all the wedding envelopes and used most of the cash to pay for the wedding. By the time we returned from our honeymoon, we had just enough money to buy a Christmas tree. The very next morning, we were back to work, ready to begin our married life together.

At Winchester Western, I encountered monthly challenges in collecting data and interpreting financial reports, largely due to my lack of formal accounting training. It became evident that Winchester was experiencing financial losses. Alongside my accounting responsibilities, I was also tasked with marketing duties, including forecasting the end of the Vietnam War. Winchester relied heavily on revenue from M16 ammunition sales during the conflict, so my role involved projecting that the conflict would continue into the 1970s, which indeed proved to be the case.

One of my primary responsibilities involved updating the pricing of Winchester Western Trap & Skeet Shooting Equipment Catalog. However, I encountered resistance from the sales team, who viewed trap and skeet equipment as loss leaders. Despite recognizing the potential benefits of updating the catalog, I faced pushback from both the sales team and management due to delays completing what seemed like a straightforward task.

Feeling frustrated and out of my depth, I decided to take matters in my own hands. Despite my lack of experience in the industry, I reached out to a competitor, Remington Arms in Bridgeport, Connecticut. Having been in and out of Remington Arms buildings while working for the Stuart L. White Company, I felt somewhat familiar with their operations.

I grabbed a phone book and dialed the main number for Remington Arms. After requesting to be patched through to the Financial Analysis Group, the call was answered immediately because it was an internal call. I introduced myself as 'Tim O'Grady, Financial Analysis' with inquiries about Trap & Skeet pricing. I was transferred over to someone who was very helpful. They walked me through the methods and the setting of various price discounts.

Armed with this newfound knowledge, I applied the same pricing formulas used by Remington Arms to Winchester equipment. I produced the suggested equipment repricing with retail, wholesale discount schedules.

The Winchester sales force postponed the printing of the new/revised catalog due to the suggested price increases. Shortly after, I received a call from the Winchester Western Corporate Office, inquiring about my contact with Remington Arms. To my surprise, I found myself in hot water. When questioned about my actions, I explained that I received no help with pricing internally, so I reached out to Remington for assistance. Management to Tim: No more marketing calls!

At the same time, I found myself entangled in a bit of trouble due to Jimmy Zambrano's memos. Jim, who was nearing retirement, occupied an office on our floor, and I could not help but notice that his memo inbox remained conspicuously empty. In the absence of email, I devised a method to ensure that he received memos by adding 'Zambrano' to my copy list.

As I was the newest person on the floor, I had to copy everyone. Nobody really paid attention to who received a copy, and so Zambrano, J. was being copied on return memos. One day I stopped by Jim's office and noticed the memos in his inbox. He was surprised at first but happy to finally receive the memos.

Someone squealed and I had to talk to—apologize to—Jim who was really pleased with my effort, but he warned me that I would be punished by being 'volunteered' for the annual November Winchester New Haven factory parts inventory. This task was known to be tedious because it involved counting parts on every factory floor over the entire weekend.

As I worked through the inventory assignment, it became increasingly clear to me that the firearm inventory was reaching its maximum capacity. My regular accounting duties had already highlighted declining firearm sales, resulting in decreasing revenue and rising costs due to ongoing accumulation of inventory. Moreover, tensions were brewing between management and the union, with talk of a potential strike circulating among employees. I knew a strike would last until the firearms inventory cleared, which would make it a long strike.

My first New Year's resolution was to find a job in 1969. My last day at Winchester Western was Friday May 2, 1969. The Winchester strike started on July 16, 1969, and ended on February 9, 1970.

My first professional job had lasted eight months.

6

# A LATER START IN LIFE HELPED MY SUCCESS

My second professional job that involved wearing a suit and tie started on Monday May 5, 1969, in Waterbury Connecticut at the Trust Department at Colonial Bank & Trust Company. I still have a copy of the Colonial Bank & Trust ad that ran in the New Haven Register: Assistant Securities Trader "Successful candidate will have significant securities experience and a strong interest in continuing his personal advancement and development." I assume Colonial used the New Haven Register to attract Yale graduates. I answered the ad and talked myself into my first visit to Waterbury.

During the interview, it became apparent that the bank's representative lacked a fundamental understanding of the assistant stock trading role. I had prepared myself for what a stock trader did, so I was able to embellish "my faux experience" to fit the narrative. My ability to think on my feet and present myself creatively stems from my childhood, which was shaped by my mother's stern demeanor. She allowed little room for humor or flexibility and would often discipline my brother Tom and me with a stick. Over time, I learned to harness this creativity and turned it into a valuable asset that served me well in unexpected situations.

Initially, I had no luck as a securities background was a requirement. However, a few months later, I received an unexpected call at home. I was offered the job at $6800 a year, starting on May 5$^{th}$. Circumstances appeared to have shifted: the first two qualified candidates with extensive securities experience had quit, and the second hire did not even finish the day. I started immediately with no time off or vacation.

My tenure at Colonial Bank lasted precisely fifteen years from the day I started, during which I was fortunate to be promoted twelve times. My father expressed surprise at my decision to join an institution based in Waterbury, considering the city's diminishing stature as the 'Brass Capital of the World'. Reflecting on Waterbury's decline, I initially failed to recognize how this decline presented unique opportunities that I would lever to my advantage.

Despite being a small regional northwest bank serving the Central Naugatuck valley with assets of $283 million, Colonial Bank & Trust's Trust Department boasted a remarkable achievement: it ranked among the top 100 in the nation. This success was largely attributed to the wealth created by the brass industry.

On my first day at the job, I quickly understood why the two experienced individuals had resigned. Instead of the dynamic role of an Assistant Trader I had envisioned—standing up with phones in both ears, barking orders to NYSE floor traders—I found myself primarily tasked with bookkeeping duties. No trading was involved. My expectation of being in the thick of the action starkly contrasted with the reality of simply keeping the books.

Senior Trust Investment Officers devised a concise one-page stock trading program. At the top of the document, they listed stocks slated for sale along with projected proceeds. Below they outlined the stocks to be purchased with the anticipated proceeds.

Once finalized, the program was sent to the client for review and authorization. Upon its return, it crossed my desk.

My responsibility was to verify the availability of stocks slated for sale that were actually in the client's account to be sold and ensure that the listed stock prices were up to date. To accomplish this, I utilized the Quotron, a stock ticker machine that provided real-time updates on New York Stock Exchange (NYSE) prices. Once confirmed, I would pass the program on to the trader for execution. This role required a level of expertise in securities trading.

During times when the trader was unavailable, whether on lunch break or otherwise occupied, I seized the chance to monitor individual portfolio performances using the Quotron machine. Having memorized the stock symbols, I delved into market trends and directions to stay informed and proactive. In the absence of my superior, I practically wore out the Quotron machine, eager to glean insights and make informed decisions.

Another major responsibility of my role involved tracking down stocks that had been sold but not yet delivered, as well as those that had been purchased but not yet received. This task was especially crucial given the complexities and potential pitfalls of the stock trading process.

When I began working at Colonial, the New York Stock Exchange (NYSE) closed on Wednesdays, which allowed an additional weekday for staff to work through the paperwork backlog. However, in 1971, U.S. Attorney General John Mitchell (remember Watergate) testified before a U.S. Senate hearing, estimating that organized crime syndicates had stolen $400 million worth of securities. Additionally, approximately one in six NYSE member firms either closed or merged during a two-year period in the late 1960s.

Lorraine and I lived in the center of Milford where our duplex was a two-hour journey by Metro-North train, followed by the #6 subway line at Grand Central Station leading down to Wall Street.

This commute required a round-trip train ticket during peak hours and two subway tokens for each trip. For lunch, I often indulged in a couple of hot dogs from the street vendors.

Despite the distance, I eagerly volunteered to visit as many Wall Street firms' operations departments as possible to facilitate the clearing of our stock trades. These visits allowed me to cultivate numerous operational contacts and successfully expedite Colonial pension stock clearing processes. Additionally, I prioritized visits to Wall Street broker trading desks to gather trading insights and information.

The opportunity to travel to New York City so frequently arose as a result of my proactive volunteering. This level of engagement and initiative would not have been feasible if I had relocated to Waterbury when I initially accepted the job offer. As I became increasingly proficient in clearing stock trades, my travels to NYC only multiplied, reflecting the growing success of my endeavors.

Now that I was considered an 'investment person', my mother sought my expertise to evaluate her Donahue Sales/Textron Pension Plan Employee investment performance. Eager to impress her, I enlisted the help of the four Colonial Trust Investment Officers to conduct a thorough review. Comparing the performance of Textron's retirement equity plan to Colonial Trust equity returns revealed a significant disparity, with Colonial's far outstripping Textron's.

The Trust Officers provided me with detailed notes on the stock issues within the Textron Plan, along with the names and addresses of the Pension personnel at Textron Headquarters in Providence, RI. Armed with this information, I compiled a comprehensive report for my mother. Unbeknownst to me, she forwarded my Colonial notes directly to the Textron Pension Investment team, copying Textron CEO, G. William Miller.

This action inadvertently stirred up some trouble, as my mother's Donahue Sales manager received backlash for sending such correspondence directly to Textron Headquarters. Apparently, it was frowned upon for employees to comment on investment performance. However, this incident led to an unexpected encounter later in life, as I had the opportunity to meet G. William Miller, Chairman of the Federal Reserve Bank, during a Federal Reserve Board meeting in Washington DC and at a presentation in Connecticut. Surprisingly, G. William Miller did not remember my mother's earlier correspondence!

Then I got lucky. In December 1969, Colonial Bank & Trust of Waterbury acquired Brooks Bank & Trust of Torrington, Connecticut. Bernhard (Ben) Hoffmann, who led Brooks Bank's Trust division, joined Colonial Trust in January 1970 as the new Head of the Trust, replacing Charlie Hall. This change prompted the retirement of Foster G. Woods, Senior Vice President, and Chairman Investment Committee, followed by Edward G. Hazen, Executive Vice President, and Chairman of the Trust Committee, the following year.

Prior to Ben's arrival at Colonial, he met with individual members of the Trust staff, including myself. During our meeting, Ben inquired about my career aspirations and what I needed to succeed. He expressed his intention to implement changes in investment operations and responsibilities, encouraging me to remain with the company and grow under his leadership. True to his word, Ben initiated the promised changes and promoted me to Securities Trader in January 1970, marking my first promotion.

Upon assuming my new role as Securities Trader, I introduced notable changes to the trading process. While I adhered to the standard procedure of selling stocks in the morning, I refrained from executing buys in the afternoon. With the stock market experiencing a downward trend, I believed it was prudent to wait for lower prices before making additional or new purchases. I consolidated same-stock sales into a single sell order which provided better pricing. Furthermore, I began depositing the cash proceeds from stock sales into newly opened (by me) savings accounts at Waterbury Savings or Naugatuck Savings Bank, temporarily earning a 5% interest rate until I deemed the stock market had bottomed out. Me —the stock market expert!

The graph below illustrates the performance of the S&P 500 Stock Index throughout 1970, depicting a downturn of -24% from January to June, with the market recovering and closing the year at a modest +0.1% year-to-date.

However, amidst these strategic maneuvers, I made a significant error by failing to execute a buy order for International Flavors & Fragrances (ticker: IFF). While other stocks on the Colonial Buy List continued to decline, IFF experienced an increase. This highlights the importance of vigilance and attention to all investment opportunities.

When I realized my mistake, I did not panic. Instead, I took responsibility and immediately reported my error to the Trust Investment Officers. We gathered in the Trust conference room to discuss what had happened and what my role entailed.

Despite the initial setback caused by my error, positive outcomes emerged for me. One was the realization that combining the purchases and sales of same stocks was a smart strategy, which resulted in better pricing and saving on broker commissions. This policy was implemented going forward.

In retrospect, I realize I should have consulted with the Trust Officers before making those decisions, as they felt their authority was being undermined. However, the advantages of securing better pricing for customers outweighed the discomfort caused by my actions, albeit marginally. As a result, I was invited to Trust Investment meetings, excluding clients, to gain insight into company addition and removals from the Trust Buy list. Additionally, I participated in Broker Research meetings where I interacted with visiting Wall Street stock research firms. The Trust Investment team's acceptance of me and my involvement in these meetings marked a significant advancement in my career.

Progress often brings challenges, and I faced one when senior management at Colonial Bank received complaints from both Waterbury and Naugatuck Savings Banks regarding my actions. They were especially concerned about my decision to deposit what they perceived as 'hot money' into their banks—funds that were expensive (earning 5%) and temporary, expected to leave once the stock market recovered.

The steep decline in the stock market, amounting to a -24% decrease in six months, reflected a slower economy and reduced demand for loans. This exacerbated the issue of excess liquidity. Unbeknownst to me, uninvested Trust cash, which I was moving to 5% savings accounts at other banks was typically sold in the overnight Federal Funds market, which benefited Colonial Bank. My actions disrupted this process and created friction within the bank. But the Trust customers loved me!

Furthermore, my inclination toward trading more in New York City rather than locally may have contributed to the reluctance of Waterbury brokers and bankers to engage with me socially. I was never asked to play golf with them at the exclusive private Waterbury Country Club.

The Trust Department trading desk was simple—just a desk, telephone and Compucorp machine. Notably, the phone had a direct line to the prestigious New York City brokerage firm Goldman Sachs, thanks to their Partner Colin Ferenbach. Colin and I developed a rapport, which facilitated communication and exchange of market insights. He generously shared his expertise and even invited me to join the Goldman team on the floor of the New York Stock Exchange several times. These experiences provided invaluable firsthand exposure to the intricacies of NYSE trading and deepened my market understanding.

I saw Dan Desmond of NYC based Rider Pyne Kendall & Hollister because Dan's parents lived at Heritage Village, a local Southbury, Ct. retirement village. Additionally, I had the opportunity to meet with Pat Young, Partner, and Head of Equity Trading at Neuberger Berman, as well as Roy Neuberger, the co-founder of the firm. I tried to talk to Pat, Colin, or Dan as frequently as possible, recognizing the importance of tapping into their expertise to bolster the Trust trading position.

In light of the changing landscape of brokerage commissions, which transitioned from fixed to negotiated stock commissions after 1968, I redirected my focus toward New York City brokers. I discovered that these brokers provided valuable street and monetary insights and were more receptive to negotiating brokerage commissions, which increased their relevance as partners for my trading strategy.

Bill Bane, a broker I met, worked at Weeden & Co. Weeden's status as a non-member of the New York Stock Exchange set it apart. Instead of public trading, Weeden specialized in making markets in specific securities, taking positions, and managing risks associated with individual stock issues. Weeden's unique approach, its innovative business model, and any potential implications for trading strategies fascinated me.

During my visits to NYC, I had the opportunity to meet with Bill Bane and the co-owners of Weeden—Don and Allen. They consistently encouraged me to consider working with them until I finally decided to give them a chance. This decision arose when I was presented with a significant order to sell 40,000 shares of Anaconda stock.

Anaconda Company, based in Waterbury, encountered substantial difficulties in the early 1970s following the nationalization of U.S. corporations and the copper industry by the re-elected Chilean President Salvador Allende. This action resulted in the loss of major affiliates in Chile and the weakening of Anaconda's financial standing. Many Trust customers held significant amounts of Anaconda stock, which prompted Colonial Trust Investment officers to swiftly assemble a sell list totaling 40,000 shares. My instructions were to liquidate the stock gradually and exercise caution throughout the process.

I contacted Weeden & Co. about their ability to trade Anaconda stock, and to my surprise, they confirmed they did. Without asking if I wanted to buy or sell, they offered a net price of $28 per share, with no brokerage commissions. They agreed to take the entire lot of 40,000 shares without hesitation.

After completing the sale, I promptly informed Ben Hoffmann, the Head of Trust, about the transaction. Recognizing Weeden's reputation and capabilities, he calculated the total proceeds of the sale and acknowledged Weeden's ability to handle the trade smoothly.

Despite the success of the trade, Ben cautioned me about potential repercussions, as the trade would not appear on the NYSE stock ticker tape due to Weeden's non-member status. Periodically, Trust personnel checked Quotron on the Anaconda stock price which showed little movement in price or volume. Eventually, I had to permit Weeden to disclose the seller's identity as a large New England Trust Company.

I was promoted once again, this time to the role of Bank Investment Portfolio Manager at Colonial Bank. This opportunity arose when the previous manager resigned to pursue a job in Boston, and

Bank management selected me to fill the position. Crucially, this promotion coincided with the deregulation of global financial markets and institutions. It marked a significant shift in the financial landscape that continues to shape the industry today.

The era of deregulation paved the way for investment managers to establish independent firms in investment management and pension consulting. Notable entries during this period included Callan Associates, Wilshire Associates, and Cambridge Associates contributing significantly to pension consulting. Additionally, Pacific Investment Management (PIMCO) and Western Asset Management emerged as two of the largest bond managers. Ray Dalio's journey began with the founding of Bridgewater Associates, which has grown into the world's largest hedge fund after starting from his humble two-bedroom apartment.

During this period, significant legislative changes occurred in retirement savings. Congress passed the Employee Retirement Income Security Act (ERISA) which introduced individual retirement accounts (IRAs) as a retirement savings option for workers without employer-sponsored retirement plans. In 1978, Congress enacted Internal Revenue Code Section 401(k) as part of the Revenue Act, revolutionizing retirement planning by offering individuals more flexibility and control over their retirement savings.

According to the Investment Company Institute, 401(k) plans hold $7.4 trillion in assets as of December 31, 2023, in more than 710,000 plans, serving approximately seventy million active participants, as well as numerous former employees and retirees. This massive pool of assets created a significant demand for pension consulting and investment management services, reflecting the pivotal role that 401(k) plans play in retirement savings and wealth management.

While initially unaware of the opportunities presented by legislative changes, I eventually realized their potential for success in finance and securities. I leveraged my skills and knowledge to gain a competitive edge in the market, committed to establishing and maintaining my position in the industry.

Managing a bank's investment portfolio, which typically represented about one-third of its total assets, was a significant responsibility. At Colonial Bank, with assets totaling around $300 million, this meant overseeing a portfolio worth approximately $100 million.

In the 1970s, only a handful of bank portfolio managers actively traded bonds to enhance returns. The dominant approach was the bond ladder strategy, which involved purchasing and holding securities with maturities ranging from one to five years or one to ten years. This strategy is still utilized by many financial advisors today. It aims to balance risk and return across different shorter maturity dates. You can learn about bond ladders by searching on YouTube.

Despite lacking prior experience in bond trading, I was encouraged to explore avenues for enhancing returns through strategic trading of tax-exempt municipal bonds, U.S. Government securities, and U.S. Government Agency securities, assets that were entirely new to me and that I never traded before.

My second promotion relocated me to the first floor, Main Bank Office, positioned behind the CEO's office. In the 1970s the main bank floor had a long row for bank tellers and a separate area for the Senior executives. I ended up sitting near the CEO. This move increased pressure and exacerbating my smoking habit. Additionally, I received a letter from the University of Rhode Island (URI) reminding me of the impending deadline to complete my master's degree by May 1972. According to URI's schedule, the first available date for my final exams was in November 1971.

In the years prior, URI had offered two options for a master's degree: two research papers plus exams or a thesis. I opted for the former using extensive Wall Street Research, some only available to large U.S. pension plans. My URI professor was pleased. I did not know at the time that I had extensive Wall Street Research available. I regretted not choosing a thesis, as now I had to study for exams after being out of graduate school for three-and-half - years!

President Nixon's nationally televised address of August 15, 1971, in which he announced a freeze on all prices and wages and the termination of the gold standard, rocked the financial world. I worked diligently to gather Wall Street Research on the changes, spending September and October absorbing and discussing their implications for my trading strategies.

In November, I faced my exam covering Nixon's economic policies and dissolution of the Bretton Woods system. With intense focus, I tackled the Nixon-related questions until the end of the test. Luckily, most of the exam was related to Nixon's economic policies and I felt very confident. Later, I received news of my induction into the University of Rhode Island Omicron Delta Epsilon-Honors Society in Economics.

# 7

## PUSHING THE ENVELOPE

During my final thirteen years at Colonial Bank, I was part of the Treasurers Group, overseeing the treasury and financing aspects of the bank's operations. With the acquisition of eight Connecticut Banks, our group worked with Maryanne Varsalone under the leadership of Joseph Carlson II and took on the responsibility of integrating and managing treasury functions of these acquired institutions. Over time, I expanded the Treasury Group into both fee-generating and trading income functions, emphasizing our role as investors rather than traditional bankers. I was made a Vice President in 1976, Senior VP in 1979, and Treasurer in 1980. Below is a photo of me in 1976, overseeing trading and portfolio management.

Navigating the bond market in the absence of listed markets like the New York Stock Exchange or electronic trading platforms demanded a significant amount of effort and persistence. As the bank portfolio manager, I had to engage in direct

communication with banks and brokers to obtain quotes for U.S. Treasuries, Federal Agencies, and Municipal bonds. This process, known as trading 'over the counter', often required making multiple calls to ensure I received the best price possible for buying and selling securities. Any of the twenty U.S. Government Bond primary dealers receiving a request from a small bank in Waterbury, Connecticut did not seem to get anybody ready to sharpen their pencils for a quote.

Obtaining a Compucorp-Monroe Trader calculator was crucial for my work, especially when dealing with bond prices. Fixed income securities were quoted in yields, not prices. I requested a Monroe Trader when I was in the Trust Department so when the unit arrived, I took it. The Monroe Trader model is pictured below with my son Ryan at two years old calculating bond prices for me.

As the bank bond manager, I focused on acquiring only high-quality municipal bond issues for the investment portfolio considering their importance in maintaining portfolio stability and minimizing credit risk. Municipal bonds are commonly rated by major credit rating agencies such as Standard & Poor's and Moody's Investment Service, as indicated in the chart from Investopedia—shown next page. While the bank took risks with commercial, personal loans, and long-term mortgages, I focused on staying updated with current information about municipal issuance and credit changes for investment decisions and trading strategies.

| Bond Rating | | | |
|---|---|---|---|
| Moody's | Standard & Poor's | Grade | Risk |
| Aaa | AAA | Investment | Lowest Risk |
| Aa | AA | Investment | Low Risk |
| A | A | Investment | Low Risk |
| Baa | BBB | Investment | Medium Risk |
| Ba, B | BB, B | Junk | High Risk |
| Caa/Ca/C | CCC/CC/C | Junk | Highest Risk |
| C | D | Junk | In Default |

*Investopedia*

Frequent visits to Wall Street gave me insights into the technology the brokers were using. I convinced Colonial Bank management to lease a Munifacts 'news' machine, a staple in major banks, brokerage firms, and municipal bond departments across the country. This machine printed a constant stream of news related to economics, business, bids wanted on municipals, and municipal new offerings. Placed prominently on the main bank floor near the CEO's office, the Munifacts machine became an attraction, drawing bank and trust officers and bank clients who would tear off a news pieces to take away. Despite the occasional hassle of managing the printed paper, the machine provided an opportunity for interactions with CEO Frank White, which fostered a comfortable relationship between us.

As I climbed the ranks as a bank officer, Lorraine and I received invitations to the exclusive Christmas dinner hosted by Bank CEO Frank White at his home. Upon arrival for the first dinner, I discovered I was seated at Frank's table. In a bold move, when no one was looking, I exchanged my name card with someone else so I could sit next to him. Frank noticed my presence beside him, hesitated for a moment, then joined me, and we engaged in conversation throughout dinner.

Continuing my visits to Wall Street, albeit less frequently than before, I wanted to ensure I had the latest technology. I noticed Telerate Monitors, essentially a TV set on all the major trading desks. These monitors displayed channels featuring rates and prices of U.S. Treasuries and Federal Agencies. With the addition of a Telerate monitor, I no longer had to spend entire days on the phone requesting prices on from brokers; instead, they were conveniently displayed right in front of me on the screen.

I had to petition Cantor Fitzgerald/Telerate to recognize Colonial Bank of Waterbury was an active U.S. Government & Agency trader eligible to trade through their technology. Leveraging my Wall Street contacts, I secured an appointment with Cantor in their NYC office. Upon entering their office, it took about twenty minutes for my eyes to adjust to almost darkness of their trading room. Dimly lit with a green glow emanating from multiple screens on the walls and ceiling, the Cantor Fitz trading room was an eerie sight. During the meeting, I highlighted the firms I traded with and exaggerated the number and frequency of trades. Thankfully, these firms corroborated my claims, which led to Colonial Bank of Waterbury, Connecticut being granted access to use Cantor Fitzgerald pricing pages on the Telerate monitor. At that time, I believe there were four or five approved users trading electronically in New England.

Frank White, CEO had a fridge in his office. There was a back door to the chairman's office that was locked when he was in but unlocked when he was traveling. I was bringing my lunch to work and used the fridge. One day, I was being stupid and went into Frank White's office while he was away to look around. I saw his calendar with 'Things to Do' and wrote in *Promote O'Grady*. Later I thought that it may not have been a great idea, but it was too late. When Frank returned, he saw the note and came out to see me with the note in his hand. Fortunately, he was in a good mood. Lucky for me that our group moved upstairs within a few days.

The behavior of the U.S. bond market in early February 1974 aroused my suspicions. Despite no clear indicators, such as the rise in oil prices or interest rates, numerous traders were offering me unusually favorable prices on bond issues. It felt as though I had suddenly become everyone's best friend, which resembled the attention I received when I got my own car at seventeen years old. It appeared that when big city bankers or brokers wanted to sell, they turned to the banks in smaller towns like mine.

I decided to put out for sale some of my federal agency and older municipal holdings and reached out to a handful of major U.S. and brokers. JP Morgan emerged as the most aggressive bidder, purchasing all the issues I put up for sale. I mixed gains and losses to square up even. Despite my nervousness at that time, my gut instinct proved correct when interest rates surged in the following months, which led to a significant drop in the prices of the issues I had sold.

Despite complaints from JP Morgan about my action, Colonial management stood behind me. Privately, they said it was a bold move but agreed with my rationale. We discussed that if interest rates had fallen instead of rising, I had the opportunity to trade to offset the loss in income from the bonds sold. That was the narrative I presented when meeting with management.

Allowing me to take such decisive action earned me additional creditability, which enabled me to take on more responsibilities within our Treasury/Funds Group. As a result, I secured another promotion. I was blessed to have Joseph Carlson II as my boss, as he consistently supported my decisions, which contributed to my career advancement. I humorously took credit for the premature grey hair he acquired along the way.

The surge in U.S. interest rates during 1973 and 1974 posed a significant challenge, as it limited trading opportunities owing to the inverse relationship between rising yields and declining bond prices.

I created a chart using data from Salomon Brothers, the leading bond & research firm of that era. The chart displays two lines representing short-term interest rates (%): one for two-year U.S. Federal

Agency paper, and the other for 30-day commercial paper. Both these investment options were widely favored by individuals and institutions alike. The depicted interest rates ranged from below 4% to as high as 18%, illustrating the market's volatile nature during that period. This contrasts with more recent times where short-term interest rates in the U.S. hovered near zero, and even turned negative in Europe.

At the end of 1971 and into 1972, both 30-day and two-year interest rates dropped before rising in 1973 and 1974. The plunge in rates at that time resulted from the Nixon act of wage and price controls which he implemented to secure his re-election in 1972. His action along with the beginning of OPEC caused higher rates in 1973/1974 and much higher rates in 1979–1983.

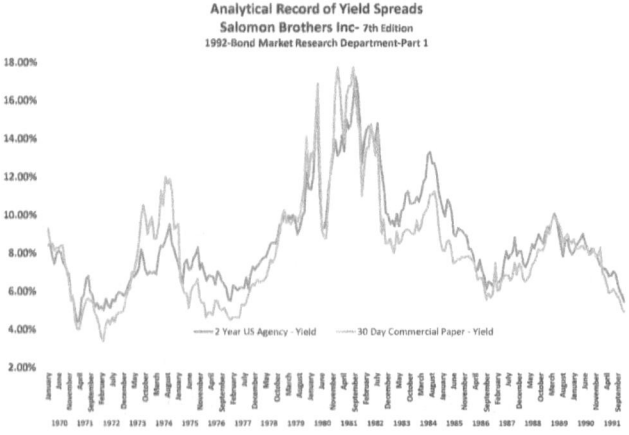

Despite the challenging market conditions, we devised another strategy to generate revenue. We identified an opportunity in the bond offerings of the U.S. Government's Federal Agencies, which consistently sought to raise short-term capital. These Federal Agency issues offered higher yields, or—in other words—higher interest rates compared to equivalent maturity U.S. Treasury issues.

However, they typically came with a minimum requirement of $100,000.

In my portfolio trading, I maintained a modest position in new Federal Agency securities usually in the range of $1–2 million. This allowed for swift trading flips when these securities were freshly issued. Together with my associate, Nancy Pierpoint, we presented a sales idea to management. The proposal involved me continuing to trade new Federal Agency issues if they were priced attractively, with a portion of the trading position allocated to our retail customers, whom we had yet to acquire.

Nancy assumed the responsibility for offering investments to bank customers, starting from a $100k minimum issue and offering various investment sizes, such as $25K, $50k, or any amount above $10k. Colonial Bank would securely hold these investments until maturity. Any unsold portions would be managed by me, assuming the risk of trading in the market. We received permission to begin slowly in 1973, but as interest rates continued to climb in 1974 (8% to 9% to 10%), our business gained traction through word of mouth.

Within a few months, we found ourselves with a queue of customers whenever a Federal Agency came to market. There were days when Nancy Pierpoint, Joe Carlson II, Al Coffey, and I were busy writing Federal Agency buy tickets non-stop. We charged a $25 fee for each purchase.

Studying Federal Reserve data was crucial for trading, as it offered insights into the impact of monetary policy on the U.S. economy. Every Thursday at 4:00 pm EDST, the Federal Reserve released an 8-page report containing statistics that were closely scrutinized by portfolio managers, traders, and investors. Deciphering 'Fed speak' and understanding Federal Reserve policy changes were valuable skills in trading any security. Pittsburgh National Bank was particularly adept at interpreting Federal Reserve data, and I am grateful to individuals like Scott Mitchell and David LeVeck for sharing their insights with me.

One of my best decisions was hiring Mark Hansen from Colonial IT. Mark was pursing graduate studies in economics at the University of Hartford, and he used his coursework to deepen his understanding of Federal Reserve policy and forecasting business cycle changes. Mark meticulously compiled a library on business cycle trend analysis, utilizing every piece of monthly economic data available. His expertise helped our trading of U.S. Government and municipal bond issues and made him the featured speaker at Colonial Bank's annual statewide Municipal Finance Conference.

Mark and I eventually traveled to Washington D.C for Federal Reserve Press Conferences on monetary policy. In 1978, we had the opportunity to meet Federal Reserve Chairman Arthur Burns while riding in his elevator. Although his handlers seemed apprehensive, the chairman took our presence in stride, and we commended him on his performance at the press conference.

In 1979, Mark and I returned to see G. William Miller, the New Federal Reserve Chairman, who was formerly the CEO of Textron in Providence, Rhode Island. During the meeting, I found myself seated next to an executive whom I knew from Bear Stearns, a large and aggressive NYC bond dealer.

As G. William Miller began his presentation on Federal Reserve Policy results, I noticed inconsistencies in the dates presented on the slides. The starting dates on the exhibits did not match, which created inconsistency in the overall presentation. I raised this issue with my friend who acknowledged that different time starts could be misleading. Our discussion grew louder, attracting attention at the meeting.

A Federal Reserve guard approached us to inquire about the disturbance. I voiced my concern about the inconsistent presentation, but the guard was indifferent. He warned me that if I did not quiet down, I would be removed. Interestingly, he addressed his warning to me and not to my executive buddy. Despite my attempts to garner support from him, he remained silent and avoided engaging with me. This is the same executive that served President Trump's administration.

Part of my responsibilities in Municipal Finance Advisory involved bidding on short-term tax- exempt notes issued by local Connecticut municipalities, especially those towns/cities we advised. At our peak, Colonial advised thirty-four municipalities. Colonial Bank's municipal finance team always kept me informed and encouraged aggressive bidding on our customer notes, which ensured that we either secured them or looked competitive in the process. These notes became part of my short-term bank portfolio because I had no customers to sell the notes to.

One day, Hartford National Bank (HNB) began aggressive bidding statewide on municipal short- term notes, extending beyond their own client relationships. Through my sources I learned that HNB was aiming to expand their Municipal Finance Department, thereby potentially taking business away from Connecticut Bank & Trust (CBT), the largest bank in Connecticut. Given Colonial's strong coverage of our clients, we were not concerned about losing clients, but I saw an opportunity to compete.

Observing HNB's bidding strategy, I decided to bid on municipalities where Colonial was not a financial advisor, which comprised the majority of the state. Our Municipal Finance Department was excited about this new market opportunity. Although I strategically refrained from purchasing any notes, I tried to consistently place second or third in the bidding process, and I came close to winning multiple times.

As questions from the press arose about Colonial's increased involvement in bidding on municipal notes, Frank White, CEO, sought an explanation. I informed Frank that it was a marketing initiative to enhance exposure for our Municipal Finance Group.

However, I had not discussed with him my broader aim of establishing Colonial as a dominant player in the tax-exempt note market in Connecticut or me as the master of the local municipal note universe. Frank preferred that I focus on management rather than on Master of Marketing initiatives.

The increased municipal note bidding had a significant ripple effect. Municipalities that we bid on began reaching out to Colonial for Certificate of Deposit (CD) offerings for their short-term investment. Suddenly, we had access to statewide short-term cash investments ranging from thirty to ninety days, allowing us to continuously roll over the cash. This provided Colonial with a stable base of cash to invest in higher-yielding short-term securities, thereby expanding our bank liability management efforts. Mark Hansen played a crucial role in managing the bidding process for the CDs, ensuring that our short-term assets and liabilities remained balanced while providing a positive return.

I thought our next step in the evolution of trading and fee generating business was to establish a dedicated Connecticut Municipal Bond Department within our Portfolio/ Treasurers Group. While I managed and traded municipal bonds for the bank's investment portfolio, I had not traded or invested in local Connecticut municipal bonds due to their smaller size, which lacked the liquidity for the bank's portfolio. However, I recognized the value in these investments and saw potential in establishing a specialized department to focus on them.

Drawing on my experience in the Colonial Trust Department, where I observed the demand for tax-free bonds among Connecticut investors, I recognized an opportunity to capitalize on this demand. Municipal bonds offered federal tax-free benefits, and income from Connecticut municipal bonds was also tax-free within the state. I proposed expanding our Treasury Group to establish a dedicated Municipal Bond Group focusing on Connecticut municipalities.

I made one of my toughest hires and brought on Bob McAllister, as I recognized his strong sales skills despite his prickly personality, which I knew would pose a challenge. After obtaining approval with the understanding that any management issues would result in both Bob and me being replaced, we offered positions to both Bob and his secretary Janet.

For the first time, there was no need to acquire any new bond technology since we had what we needed. All we required was a copy of the Daily Blue List of Municipal Bond offerings, which provided an inventory of available municipal bond issues. Negotiating with the publisher to have the Blue List delivered to Colonial Bank in Waterbury early each morning took a few weeks, with the publisher initially puzzled by our request for delivery to Waterbury, Connecticut.

Bob proved to be diligent, and arrived early to scour the Blue List for bargains before anyone else had their coffee. Together, Bob and Janet excelled in building up Colonial's Connecticut Municipal Bond Department, garnering a significant following in New England.

In a bold step forward, in April of 1975, I orchestrated Colonial Bank's participation in a municipal underwriting group led by Chase Manhattan & First Pennco Securities for a $140 million Commonwealth of Pennsylvania municipal issue. While Colonial Bank nor I were ever involved in municipal underwriting, I saw an opportunity to capitalize on the attractive potential yields of the Commonwealth of Pennsylvania bonds.

With some persuasive efforts, I managed to secure Colonial's inclusion in the Chase/Pennco bidding syndicate, leveraging my connections with Joseph McManus and Miles Slater at First Pennco Securities. As a portfolio manager, I reserved some four-year and five-year bonds pre-sale for a portfolio investment. My strategy was to hold onto the bonds until maturity unless interest rates declined materially allowing me to sell the Pennsylvania bonds at a nice gain.

The trade proved profitable as the underwriting sold out completely and the over the summer interest rates declined so I sold the Penn holdings. The underwriting check was much bigger than I thought.

However, the trade came with its share of challenges, particularly in the form of unexpected attentions after Colonial's involvement was advertised in publications like the Wall Street Journal and New York Times (see below).

Seeing the unexpected response to the advertisement, I realized it was time to face Frank White, the Bank CEO, as I knew I stretched my responsibilities involving Colonial in municipal underwriting activities. I was no longer an underwriter.

Levering my connections with major NYC bank and broker municipal underwriters, I sought permission from Colonial management to submit syndicated bids for State of Connecticut bond offerings on behalf of these underwriters. Typically, I approached underwriters like Citibank, Salomon Brothers, or Chase ahead of time to request permission to represent them at the auction in Harford, CT, instead of their own representatives driving up from NYC.

Operationally, the underwriter would send me their bid form with the Net Interest Cost (NIC) column left blank. Prior to the auction, I traveled to Hartford and stationed myself near a phone booth close to the Capital. From there, I called the NYC syndicate contact and gave him the phone number. They typically responded with the NIC just minutes before the deadline. After receiving the NIC, I meticulously recorded it, repeated it for accuracy, sealed the envelope, and rushed to the auction meeting at the Capital to present the bid to State Treasurer Henry Parker on behalf of the underwriter. The bid, complete with a timestamp and meeting the deadline, was then considered for acceptance.

Connecticut newspapers had Colonial Bank submitting the winning bid for the underwriters. If we were not the winning bid, Colonial Bank would be mentioned: "other bidders included the Colonial Bank Group-and leading underwriter".

Eventually, I passed the responsibility to the Colonial Municipal Finance Department. The NIC bid usually came in at the last minute with someone screaming numbers and me running to make the deadline. I came close one too many times. I am not a fast runner. I can jump like a gazelle but cannot run.

The financial turmoil in New York City during the mid-1970s garnered widespread attention. President Gerald Ford's speech on October 29, 1975, where he refused federal assistance to prevent New York City from declaring bankruptcy, made headlines across the nation. The stark headline on the front page of the Daily News on October 30, 1975, captured the sentiment: "FORD TO CITY: DROP DEAD."

To prevent future municipal financial crises, the Municipal Securities Rule Making Board (MSRB) established regulations. I was granted waivers for membership exams, MSRB #52, MSRB #53 from Ella Grasso, Governor of the State of Connecticut. She learned about my work bidding on local Connecticut town municipals notes and the State of Connecticut Bond issues and granted the waivers without us ever meeting or speaking directly to me.

I sought a dedicated municipal bond manager to oversee the

banks' municipal bond portfolio, a role I had initially handled alongside other expanding responsibilities within our investment group. Recognizing the need for someone with expertise in longer-term municipal bond management, we aimed to find a candidate similar to David Eurkus of CBT known for his prowess in the market. Interestingly, David Eurkus approached us one day and expressed his awareness of our search and interest in the position. After discussions, we extended the offer, and despite being a prominent figure in municipal bond world, David Eurkus opted to join our team in Waterbury.

In 1976, our team solidified, and it proved to be our best year yet in terms of trading and sales, fueled by a gradual decline in interest rates. While larger banks like CBT, HNC, the Bank of Boston, and the Industrial Bank of Rhode Island loomed in New England, none could match our expertise in both taxable and municipal bonds. Despite our smaller size, we proved that quality outweighed quantity, thereby establishing ourselves as a formidable force in the regional banking landscape.

In 1981, the City of Waterbury found itself with a surplus of several million dollars, a rare occurrence, possibly attributable to a mild winter that saved costs on snow plowing and street maintenance. Seizing this opportunity, I proposed a program for the city to invest in deeply discounted U.S. Government securities. These securities would then be used to collateralize an existing municipal bond issue, effectively removing its impact on the city's balance sheet. By implementing the collateralization strategy, the city could positively influence its financial standing over the coming years.

After presenting the plan to the City of Waterbury for review and approval, complete with a list of U.S. Treasuries to purchase, it was executed by Connecticut Bank & Trust Company of Hartford (CBT), the new financial advisor for the city. Waterbury Mayor Mike Bergin had been upset years earlier when he was told that the Colonial Bank investment portfolio did not own any Waterbury bonds. I knew he was upset but I thought I squared up with him on the municipal defeasance/collateralization idea.

In October 1981, Colonial Bank launched a new deposit account called the Money Market N.O.W. (Negotiable Order of Withdrawal). This account, backed by U.S. Treasury securities held in our investment portfolio, offered checking with interest. Its introduction aimed to replace higher cost purchased funds and generate fees. The response was immediate, with $60 million raised swiftly. Despite objections from Bank America, Colonial Bank's CEO and Joseph Carlson II stood firm on our name. Offering interest on a checking account was a pioneering and significant innovation in the field of banking services.

Waterbury Mayor Mike Bergin called me just before I left Colonial Bank. He took me to lunch at Diorio's Italian Restaurant on Bank Street and wished me luck. I was worried when a police car showed up at the bank with a driver to take us to lunch just down the street. We left as friends.

# 8

## STARTING OVER AGAIN

In early 1980, I leveraged my market connections with Bill Richardson at Donaldson Lufkin & Jenrette (DLJ) to attend a one-week business management class at the Yale School of Management (SOM) in New Haven. The course centered on power-sharing among senior executives, with management forming a cabinet and collectively assuming responsibilities. This concept intrigued me and I saw it as a potential pathway for career advancement.

Colonial implemented the cabinet concept when I was promoted to Bank Treasurer in June 1980. However, the intended sharing of responsibilities did not materialize as expected. Instead, there was a proliferation of committees and discussions, which led to numerous promotions but little tangible action. Nevertheless, my role as treasurer did afford me more authority.

The beginning of the end of Colonial Bank & Trust Company can be traced back to a London-based international lending initiative in 1973. Colonial's management recognized the limited growth potential in Connecticut and made the decision to expand into international lending as a strategic move. Or something like that.

The establishment of the London branch in 1981 marked a major milestone in Colonial's international expansion efforts. It was a significant endeavor involving the set-up of a sizable staff of twenty-one people including a cook who had previously served the queen of England. To commemorate the opening of the London office, Colonial created solid brass paper weights made from Waterbury Brass. One of the solid brass paperweights fell into my pocket and is pictured below.

In 1982, the Colonial International (London Office) suffered a significant setback, losing $28 million on a loan portfolio concentrated on Greek shipping. The substantial loss seriously depleted Colonial's equity base. In response, on December 17, 1982, First National Bank of Boston injected $25 million in new capital to bolster Colonial's financial position.

In my mind, it was evident that with Federal Reserve regulations and the changing landscape of interstate banking, larger banks were gearing up to expand across state lines to absorb smaller ones. The infusion of capital from First National Bank of Boston into Colonial Bank underscored this shift, which signaled the onset of consolidation within the banking sector. It was this realization that prompted my desire to exit the banking industry.

In the spring of 1982, I began my MBA journey by enrolling in a business class at the University of New Haven. Fate intervened when my professor recommended the Executive Management Degree (EXMBA) program, tailored for seasoned professionals with a decade of management experience. With a rigorous curriculum spanning twenty courses over two ten-month semesters, punctuality and attendance were non-negotiable. Colonial Bank promptly paid the $10,000 fee upon acceptance, allowing me to begin my studies in September 1983.

The merger of Colonial Bank into the First National Bank of Boston on April 12, 1984, marked a pivotal moment in both banking history and in my personal journey. Colonial Bank narrowly missed being the first cross-state bank acquisition. I submitted my resignation just before the merger announcement—effective May 5, 1984, my 15$^{th}$ anniversary—to ensure a smooth transition.

On May 3, 1984, Colonial Bank had a heartfelt going away-party for me at the Waterbury Club, an exclusive business club in town. The highlight of the event was a touching moment captured in a photo: me alongside Joseph Carlson II, my boss and my sponsor throughout my years, at the bank.

It was a joyous occasion, and I was deeply touched by the gesture.

On my first day of my EXMBA class, I ran into Denis Pilch, whom I recognized from his tenure at the Second New Haven National Bank, which Colonial had acquired in 1976. Denis introduced me to colleagues Dayle Sheridan and Tom Lilburn, all senior Southern New England Telephone (SNET) executives. Our inaugural class was taught by M.L. McLaughlin, Ph.D., who later ascended to the role of Dean, College of Business, Director of the EXMBA program.

The two pictures following were taken in December 1983 by my classmate Noel Tomas, who was the UNH news bureau director and editor of UNH Insight. We hired a belly dancer to celebrate the end of classes for 1983.

The first picture is me holding the class book—*Introduction to Management Economics*, next to the dancer with "An Economics Lesson" written on her belly, and the University of New Haven Graduate professor for our EXID 918 Managerial Economics class.

In the second picture left to right: Ron Buchanan, Robert Baxter (a younger person who was in class for only a few weeks), then me with my curly hairdo, Denis Pilch (on my left just behind the dancer), Sheldon Dill, Sam Bergami, John Burke ("the belly dancer helper"), last pictured on the far right is Brian Clarke.

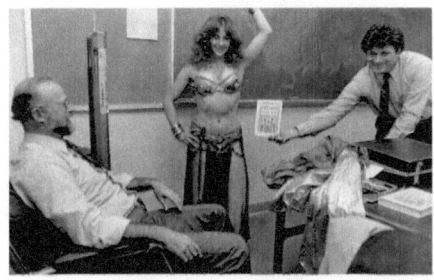

A year after graduation, Lorraine and I watched Brian Clarke race his stock car at Lime Rock Park in Lakeville, CT. Brian, a rookie, had built the car while working at Sensor Engineering. Despite his newcomer status, Brian won Rookie of the Year at the Lime Rock Race. It brought back memories of actor Paul Newman racing there years prior.

In May 1988, Sam Bergami and Brian Clarke invited me to play in the Connecticut Irish Open, which benefited a University of Bridgeport scholarship. Surprisingly, I won low gross earning a blue jacket and a putter from the event. I am still searching for a brochure to show my boys my golfing triumph.

to benefit Halsey International Scholarship Program
University of Bridgeport

9

## TWO GUYS IN HARTFORD

In search of opportunities, I focused on Connecticut to prioritize stability for my family. With the comfort that our home, friends, and schools provided, staying close was crucial. Our eldest son, Ryan, was already entrenched in his studies at the prestigious Taft High School in Watertown. Despite these responsibilities, I remained committed to my EXMBA program in New Haven, attending classes on Thursday afternoons. As I explored career options, I visited workplaces and gained valuable insights into different industries and career paths.

Bob McAllister, a colleague from our time at Colonial Bank, presented an intriguing opportunity: to join him at Roosevelt & Cross in Hartford. Both Bob and Janet departed Colonial to establish a Roosevelt & Cross office in Hartford. I was tasked with creating and leading the U.S. Government Securities Department, a new department and product for the firm.

Roosevelt & Cross did not trade, underwrite, or sell U.S. Government or Federal Agency Securities and none of the forty-six employees requested that they add U.S. Governments as a product.

Bob's persuasion paved the way for the establishment of this new department, with me in charge.

'Timothy J. O'Grady, U.S. Government Bond Department' was printed on my business cards. The excerpt below is from the New York Times May 10, 1984 (section D, page 15).

My wife Lorraine also worked with me for Roosevelt (see business card below). I developed a computer program to measure daily changes in Federal Agency and U.S. Treasury yield spreads. Each evening, I printed the closing yields for Lorraine to input into the program spreadsheet. While I was having dinner, she ran the model which I reviewed before bed. The next day, if a trading opportunity persisted, I acted upon it.

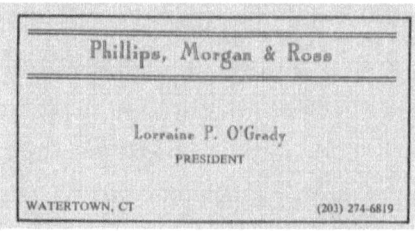

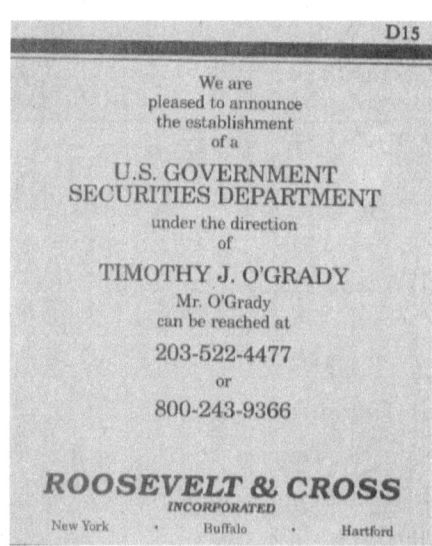

Before joining Roosevelt, I made a crucial phone call to set up the Cantor Fitzgerald application on a Telerate monitor, which enabled me to trade U.S. Government & Federal Agency securities on day one.

On Sundays I stayed with my in-laws in New Jersey for early Monday morning meetings at Roosevelt's NYC office. I took vacation days from Colonial to focus on U.S. Government and Agency Securities trading/sales with the municipal salesforce. Although we discussed expanding the U.S. Government Bond business with the Roosevelt & Cross municipal bond clients, it did not gain traction due to significant profit differences between a municipal trade and U.S. Government trade. My priority was generating income through trading to cover department costs and later develop a saleable product for the municipal team.

Securing a securities financing line from a Wall Street firm while trading was based in Hartford, Connecticut, presented a significant challenge. A firm had to finance our positions.

Before joining Roosevelt & Cross, I met with Miles Slater, a partner at Salomon Brothers who had previously assisted me during his time at First Pennco Securities in 1975. Back then, Miles helped Colonial Bank participate in the State of Pennsylvania municipal underwriting deal, despite Colonial not being an underwriter.

In late 1978 and early 1979, I invited Miles Slater to a Colonial Bank Board meeting to discuss using financial futures for interest rate hedging. Given my expanded asset and liability matching responsibilities, I believed financial futures could be valuable risk management tools. Miles brought along colleague, John F. Eckstein of JF Eckstein Securities, but despite thorough discussion, there was no rush to move to interest rate futures for hedging.

Seeking Miles's guidance once again as I transitioned to Roosevelt & Cross, he took the initiative to shepherd the request for a financing line through the Salomon Brothers Senior Management Group for approval. This resulted in securing a $20 million line of financing. The Salomon U.S. Government financing rate offered significant advantages; it was less than half of the prime lending rate offered by Bank of New York, Roosevelt's bank.

I needed an assistant or partner to help me with the phones and coverage. Roosevelt recommended Don McDonald, a senior at Princeton University, who had previously interviewed at Roosevelt's main office in New York. They provided me with Don's contact number and indicated that he was expecting my call. Don's background included internships at Salomon Brothers and Chase Manhattan Bank.

Don knew someone named Tim would be calling him, but he was unaware of the job description. I explained it was a startup U.S. Government Bond Trading/Sales Unit inside a municipal bond firm. I emphasized that there were no existing clients. The role involved trading and business development. From day one, you would be on the phone trading and making calls to brokers and reaching out to prospects. Don agreed to join me in Hartford.

In the summer of 1984, Merrill Lynch introduced an offering of TIGR's, or Treasury Investment Growth Receipts. As an underwriter, Merrill purchased a USA Treasury twenty-year bond Issue, specifically the 12 3/8% due on May 15, 2004. Using scissors—yes scissors—Merrill physically divided up the Treasury bond issue into a principal piece maturing on May 15, 1984, and six-month coupons that paid interest on May 15 and November 15 each year until May 15, 2004.

The principal piece maturing on May 15, 2004, was a zero-coupon bond since the coupons were cut off. The price of the principal is sold at a deep discount to face value but matures at face value. Since there are no coupon payments, the return on investment comes from the difference between purchase price and the face value. Zero-coupon bonds are attractive for certain types of investment accounts like Uniform Gift to Minors, KEOGH plans, and Individual Retirement Accounts (IRAs) because they offer a predictable return. TIGR principal issues sold in minimum denomination of $1k.

There was a significant demand from insurance companies for cash flows, particularly in acquiring strips of six-month U.S. Treasury bond coupons. With Don's help from his Merrill buddy, Mark Dorsett, Roosevelt & Cross joined the underwriting.

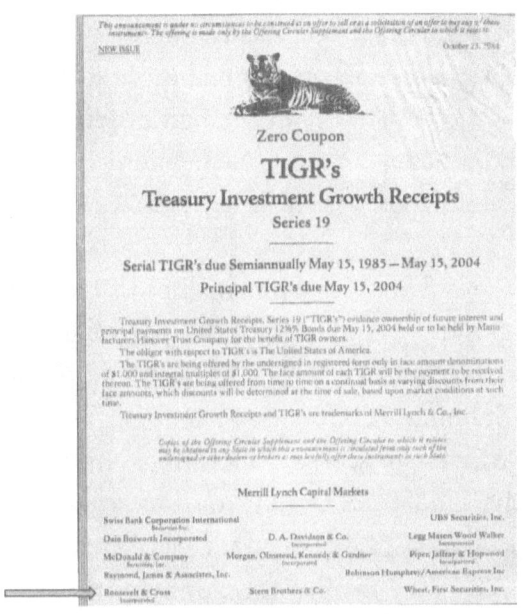

Roosevelt & Cross is listed in the New Issue Zero Coupon deal shown above. A big deal for me and Roosevelt & Cross because the municipal salesmen could get any extra fees as a result of Roosevelt & Cross being an underwriter. This was a home run.

Merrill Lynch was not the only firm involved in the creation of stripped bonds from longer-term U.S. Treasury securities. Salomon Brothers had CATS (Certificates of Accrual on Treasury Securities), and Lehman Brothers had LION (Lehman Investment Opportunity Note). Major firms, with connections to entities like lotteries and insurance companies, controlled future underwriting deals. Despite my efforts, I could not secure Roosevelt into another underwriting deal. Eventually, the U.S. Treasury itself intervened by electronically issuing U.S. Treasuries with a zero-coupon principal with six-month cash flows. This replaced intermediaries like Merrill Lynch and Salomon Brothers and Lehman Brothers.

In reflecting on those days, Don's knack for trading emerged swiftly. Together, we seized upon the Federal Reserve's easing in November 1984, a pivotal moment marked by a surge in liquidity by the Fed during the holidays because money supply shrinks a bit as checking and savings accounts are drained for holiday shopping.

I did not hit all the best trades in the first quarter of 1985 and there were some comments on how NYC municipal sales could have made more because they were just better U.S. Government bond traders.

In March 1985, my U.S. Government Bond Operation ended, marked by intense trading and significant portfolio adjustments under Mark Hansen's guidance. Mark Hansen, the Chief Investment Officer of Conning & Co., entrusted me with the helm, which allowed us to change security allocations around in several portfolios under his guidance. Despite our meticulous efforts to secure favorable prices, a wave of trade settlement complaints emanated out of NYC, which led to the closing of the operation by mid-March. Remarkably, March 1985 stands out as the pinnacle of interest rates over the past four decades—a testament to the right idea combined with impeccable timing, but at the wrong firm for the venture.

*Roosevelt & Cross Hartford Office staff—1984 In the back (left to right), is Don McDonald with Lite Beer in hand, Wally, me, and Bob McAllister. Sitting in front is Janet Everin Carta (left) and Jim Crowley. I'm not sure why we had paper on our faces or who even took the photo.*

## 10

## A FORTUNE TELLER

I returned to the market armed with my Executive MBA degree and determined to explore opportunities beyond my previous scope. I cast my net wider and extended my job search into Fairfield County and New York City. I circled a map of Connecticut, considering opportunities within a one-and-a-half-hour radius of my home in Watertown, CT.

Despite the distance, I interviewed for a pension investment position at Textron in Providence, Rhode Island. The opportunity seemed promising, but Textron's acquisition of AVCO in Stratford, Connecticut changed the situation. The AVCO pension manager was transferred to Providence, which ended my opportunity. Years later, at EAI Consulting, I participated in the search for a replacement for that pension manager.

Lorraine's visit to a fortune teller in Hamden, CT, with neighbor and friend Tricia Kropp, turned out to be surprisingly accurate. The fortune teller, known for assisting local law enforcement in locating missing persons, made several predictions for Lorraine. Among them was the foresight that her husband would secure a job at an insurance company, specifically working with computers. This revelation was particularly unexpected as insurance companies were not on my radar for potential employment, and I had been grappling with computer-related tasks.

The fortune teller's predictions did not stop there. She also assured Lorraine that we would not have to relocate, and she ominously predicted that our youngest son would be involved in a car accident. What is truly astonishing is that Lorraine had not disclosed any information to the fortune teller, leaving us astounded and contemplative.

Despite lacking any background in insurance products, I came across an intriguing job opportunity advertised in the New York Times for a position at Mutual of New York Pension (MONY PEN) in Purchase, New York. Mutual of New York—commonly known as MONY—stood as a prominent insurance company. Undeterred by my lack of experience in the industry, I applied for the position.

Purchase, New York, was situated approximately an hour and a half from my home and could be reached via a straightforward route: westward on route 84 in Connecticut transferring to route 684 south in New York, to exit 1. The MONY PEN office was right off exit 1.

In early July, I received a call for an interview with Phil Maisano, Senior Vice President, Head of Marketing/Client Service at MONY PEN. Upon meeting Phil, he candidly remarked, "Ignore the job description, you do not fit it." Perfect! The third job out of four I did not fit!

During the interview, Phil expressed his interest in finding someone with a diverse investment background to assist in expanding MONY PEN's pension product line. He asked if I had any inclination toward contributing to this endeavor within an insurance setting. I responded affirmatively, noting that starting a role without any prior experience in the industry was just part of standard operating procedure (SOP) for me.

I shared my acquaintance with Michael Drabb, Senior Vice President and Head of Investments at MONY Headquarters. I recounted my interactions with Mike during my tenure as Treasurer of Colonial Bank, where MONY had served as lender. I also mentioned my familiarity with Floyd Smith, Vice Chairman and Chief Investment Officer, whom I had met during my last visit to MONY Headquarters in 1983. I told Phil to call Mike Drabb for a reference if he had any doubts about me. Mike saw me build the Treasury Investment Group at Colonial Bank.

In the midst of awaiting a response, Lorraine made plans for an August trip to San Francisco, including Yosemite Park, accompanied by my parents and our two oldest boys Ryan and James. Lorraine said we were going, and we did. We kept checking for phone messages but there was none from MONY.

Upon returning from our vacation, I resumed my church duties, which included assisting with collections. Unlike the practices of my Catholic upbringing, we only had one collection at our church. Stepping into the church basement, known as the Rectors Room, I began the task of opening envelopes and recording the contributions, comparing them to pledges made by our congregation members. Meanwhile, my son Mark was lending a hand in the nursery, and Lorraine was busy teaching Sunday school. Before we left the church to go home for lunch, Rev Jeffrey Kittredge saw us and asked how we were doing with the job search. Money was not a problem, but I was just disappointed at not being able to secure a position. I worried I might have to move my family. After church, Jeff came to the house, talked with Lorraine and me for a long time, and then we prayed. Pictured: Jeff Kittredge and wife Silva.

The next day, a Monday, I got a call from MONY PEN and was offered a position, starting the first week in September 1985. We still talk about Jeff's visit and our prayers. Yes, I got a job at an insurance company in their pension subsidiary, and the first major product introduced was a computer driven equity program. I was called Mr. Computer Tim at MONY PEN. Christopher, my youngest son, was being taught to ride a bike by his oldest brother Ryan. One day, he took off riding. A few minutes later we got a knock on our door by the Armond's, neighbors who were all upset that they hit Chris riding his bike. Chris was ok, just a little cut on his ear. Lorraine asked Rev. Jeff about the fortune teller, but he had no answer.

Lorraine got a new art teaching position at WAMGO-Warren, Morris, Goshen Middle and High School the same day I started at MONY! Both employed.

On the morning of September 3, 1985, I stepped into the

MONY PEN offices, eager yet apprehensive about what lay ahead. My first encounter was with Gordon Perry, the commanding figure who oversaw the MONY-GPOC complex at Manhattanville, Purchase New York. Gordon, the boss of bosses, held the power to seal my fate in this new venture. Despite his absence during my August interview, his presence loomed large, and his approval was the key to my continued employment.

As I sat across from Gordon, the weight of the moment settled upon me. Every word, every gesture felt like a test. But as our conversation progressed, I found myself gaining confidence, navigating the discussion with ease. I secured Gordon's endorsement, then I was informed that I would be joining the 10:00 a.m. MONY van for a trip to New York City to MONY headquarters at 1740 Broadway, NYC to meet with Mike Drabb. Little did I know the meeting with Mike Drabb would set the tone for what lay ahead in my career at MONY.

As we approached the MONY Building, a tune unexpectedly bubbled up from me. It was the catchy melody of MONY/MONY song, a 1968 single by Tommy James and the Shondells. The song's title was inspired by Tommy James' view of the MONY sign atop the Mutual of New York Building on the New York City skyline from his Manhattan apartment. Tommy James wanted something catchy like 'Sloopy' or 'Bony Maroney', but everything sounded so stupid. When I was at Colonial Bank, every time I went to the MONY Headquarters, I could never take the executives seriously because I was humming the tune.

Upon entering Mike Drabb's office, I was met with an unexpected directive: to close the door behind me. His demeanor revealed that my presence at MONY Purchase had caught him off guard. The email he had received that morning outlined my role with extensive responsibilities, detailing my involvement with MONY's Investment Department, and Evaluation Associates Inc (EAI). It identified new product and market opportunities and served as a resource to the Pension Sales organization. As Mike processed this information, a disconnect between his expectations and the actual scope of my job became apparent. This discrepancy seemed to puzzle him, highlighting the need for clarification and alignment moving forward.

On my second day at MONY, I traveled to Westport, Connecticut to meet with Evaluation Associates Inc (EAI), which had recently joined the MONY family. Mutual of New York acquired EAI to help identify equity investment managers and products for pension investors, rather than buying a single investment management firm.

Initially, in 1984, MONY considered acquiring Townsend-Greenspan & Company but opted for EAI instead. Interestingly, Alan Greenspan of Townsend-Greenspan later became the 13$^{th}$ Chairman of the Federal Reserve in 1987.

I came across the Townsend-Greenspan news while preparing for my MONY Pension interview. I knew the firm employed twenty economists who used computer models to simulate the national economy. However, I did not see the connection between Townsend-Greenspan and MONY's needs, and I decided it was best not to ask about it during my interview.

EAI's role was pivotal in developing new pension products in alignment with MONY PEN's expansion plans. However, upon my arrival, I encountered a chilly reception from many EAI employees. It became apparent that resentment lingered among them regarding the acquisition. They had hoped to retain ownership of EAI themselves and the transition to being under the wing of a mid-size New York mutual life insurance company, accompanied by a seemingly silly song, left them disillusioned. Moreover, skepticism arose about collaborating with a former banker whom they had not previously encountered.

Months before officially commencing my role, EAI provided a list of five suggested new pension investment strategies for MONY Headquarters to potentially seed. However, none of these strategies came to fruition—they remained unfunded and unimplemented.

With the start of my position, I became a member of the Purchase Pension Investment Committee (PIC), a monthly gathering held at MONY Headquarters. Our task was to scrutinize the investment portfolios of MONY pension clients. Teaming up with John Hartz, stationed at Headquarters, we conducted thorough reviews of each client portfolio every six months and made recommendations to the committee in NYC. To streamline my effort, I acquired a portfolio optimizer, which enhanced our ability to compare different strategies and suggest changes. Remarkably, nobody had any questions about this acquisition, which was the first time I introduced a new piece of technology without any inquiries.

As expected, the Headquarters PIC Committee opted to maintain the status quo, favoring existing MONY NYC insurance investment and equity products over the suggested new strategies.

Among the five suggested strategies proposed by EAI, only one stood out as distinctly different from MONY's existing offerings to pension clients. This strategy, known as Protected Equity or portfolio insurance, utilized a computer program to calculate the required number of S&P 500 futures contracts to be sold, effectively creating an equity put option. This innovative approach aimed to establish a safeguard against potential losses in the stock market, or at the very least, mitigate them to some degree.

Amidst this period, several insurance firms, including Aetna and The Harford Company headquartered in Hartford, had already introduced guaranteed portfolio insurance products.

Having been introduced to Gifford Fong of Gifford Fong Associates (GFA) through his fixed income software programs during my tenure at Colonial Bank, I was familiar with his expertise in the field. When I discovered that he developed a portfolio insurance model, I reached out to him with an inquiry. I asked if he would consider providing MONY Purchase with both hardware and software for practice purposes, at a significantly reduced fee for a limited time. To my delight, he agreed to the proposal.

I diligently ran the technology every day—including weekends—both at the office and even on weekends at home. I arranged meetings with MONY Headquarters to present the technology, seeking their input and feedback. Additionally, I involved the MONY actuaries in the Purchase location, allowing them to examine the software and question the mathematical underpinnings behind the programs. So far, the response was positive and promising.

In May 1987, I had the opportunity to make a presentation to the MONY Purchase sales force. The picture captured here shows me at home, preparing for the upcoming meeting. I still have a recording of myself practicing for the presentation.

One of the highlights of the presentation was the demonstration of my homemade IBM computer with a screen and inserts for discs. I also created a mock exhibit featuring a three-year zero-coupon U.S. Treasury Bond—the safety asset in our equation—alongside an illustration of a 3% floor on a stock market decline. To emphasize the concept of a 'hard floor', I replaced the original 3% air filter sign with a wooden one with the intention of knocking on it with my fist during the presentation. The presentation went well. A few days later at a Group Pension meeting, I was honored to receive the GPOC Hero award for my contributions to the Protected Equity Program. The award was presented to me by none other than Jim Attwood, the esteemed Chairman of the Board of MONY.

"Tim O'Grady has been named a GPOC hero because his innovative work on portfolio insurance has vaulted us to the forefront of new investment frontiers. With the able assistance of the investment professionals in World Headquarters, we are developing expertise which should allow us to be the first New York insurer to introduce a guaranteed equity product. Clearly, this will give us a marketing advantage and enhance our reputation as an innovator in the investment business. Tim's unique ability and unbridled enthusiasm for exotic investment ideas make him a valuable resource for the pension business and a clear example of a GPOC hero."

Before the Protected Equity Program could be marketed, it

underwent thorough scrutiny by the investment and actuarial teams at the New York MONY Headquarters. Their review and subsequent sign-off on the product were crucial steps in ensuring its credibility and readiness for the market. With the support of EAI, we felt confident that we had strong allies backing our endeavor.

Our first presentation of the protected equity three-year investment took place in August 1987 at Sara Lee. Ken Levine, Chief Actuary, and I presented our proposal. I did not have a logo for Sara Lee, but Lorraine bought a box of Sara Lee cheesecake, and I copied the Sara Lee logo off the box for the cover of our presentation. The Sara Lee meeting started, then stopped abruptly when the woman in charge got up and left. She returned a few minutes later with copies of the recently approved Sara Lee logo which had not entered circulation yet. Sara Lee liked the material and preferred that we actively manage the 'put' by keeping the band or range of equity movement tight.

I was taken aback by the unexpected development with MONY Headquarters request for the Gifford Fong technology. It meant that the professionals in New York City would be responsible for managing the program, a shift from my expectations. Determined to have a role in the management of the Protected Equity program at MONY, I collaborated closely with Ken Levine, Chief Actuary, and his actuarial team at MONY Pension. After persistent efforts, we finally secured a breakthrough—a client. We decided to start after we had two small clients.

The stock market crash of October 19, 1987—famously known as Black Monday—remains a landmark event in financial history. The rapid decline in stock prices, exacerbated by the use of portfolio insurance strategies, led to widespread panic and a major disruption in financial markets.

In the years preceding the Oct 1987 crash, the Dow Jones Industrial Average saw an unprecedented surge, more than tripling in value. This exponential growth led to excessive valuation levels, indicative of an overvalued stock market (see Bloomberg graph below). Portfolio insurance gave investors a false sense of security, leading them to take on more risk than they should have. When the stock market started to decline, the rush to sell off equities to hedge against losses only served to accelerate the downward spiral.

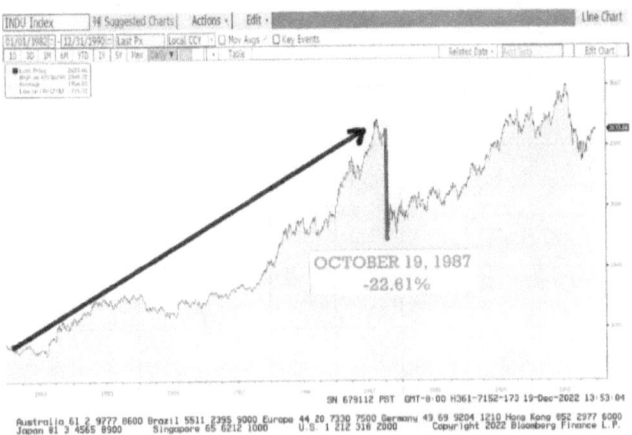

When the stock market started to decline, I called New York to assess the damage. On October 19, 1987, the computer responsible for managing the program was not operational. The investment team was relocating floors, and the technology had been unplugged in the moving process. I told them to never, *never-ever* tell anyone the technology was unplugged—never.

I took one for the team on the loss and worked with the professionals at Mutual of New York to rectify the situation. Strategic adjustments were implemented, replacing the U.S. Treasuries with higher-yielding private placements to help the clients recover their investment over the three-year period. During the three-year protected equity program time frame, the Dow Jones Industrial Average made a little over 3% for those who stayed invested in U.S. equities.

At the close of 1989, Phil Maisano, Senior Vice President and Head of Marketing MONY Purchase, departed to assume the role of President and CEO of EAI Consulting. Phil was my sponsor and mentor. Despite the changes, I found myself in a position of esteem within the MONY Pension organization. The lack of pressure from MONY to swiftly secure another position within the organization gave me freedom to explore different options and decide on my next career step.

## 11

# BUILDING FIXED INCOME RESEARCH

Securing approval for the Protected Equity product within Mutual of New York (MONY) was a significant achievement that required considerable effort and dedication. Launching a new multi-manager active bond account with EAI added another layer of complexity. However, amidst the challenges, a stroke of luck appeared. A senior MONY Purchase sales executive played a pivotal role by bringing in a new pension client, a company owned by his family. Initially, the MONY Headquarters PIC recommended the MONY private placement fixed income fund over my proposed new active multi-manager EAI bond account. However, the sales executive's recommendation of the newly managed fixed income account during his family pension meeting resulted in the client agreeing to seed the account. It felt like winning the Super Bowl.

Taking a leap with Evaluation Associates Incorporated (EAI) in Norwalk, Connecticut felt like a pivotal moment. Beyond the hope for a new opportunity, there was a practical consideration: the tax implications of my work location. Working in Connecticut allowed me to sidestep the hefty New York State taxes. I had to keep track and report my days working in Connecticut.

One of the marketing ideas for pension products was to develop a business cycle index, inspired by business cycle programs Mark Hansen used at Colonial Bank to help manage our bank portfolio investments. I purchased a copy of the ITR Economics cycle indicator program Mark used at Colonial. My idea was to create a MONY or EAI ELF index, modeled after the popular 'elves' segment on the TV show *Wall Street Week with Louis Rukeyser*. On the show, technical analysts, known as 'elf', attempted to predict the stock market and economic trends (+/-). The show became popular because of the elves' frequent prediction inaccuracies. Given their low success rate, we would not be under much pressure to achieve high accuracy, which could make our index an interesting low-stakes addition to our marketing strategy.

I failed to create an EAI or MONY ELF index because I lacked the math skills to organize and sift through the weekly/monthly data, and I was not offered any help.

Engaging with Evaluation Associates initiated deep discussions surrounding asset allocation to market EAI/MONY multi-manager funds. However, the project was temporarily set aside when I pursued the Protected Equity Program. I was drawn by its promises of security and growth.

Upon revisiting the asset allocation project, a significant shift had occurred. An EAI Group, with the first of its kind $2 billion Managed GIC Fund, departed to establish their own venture. This opened the door for me to push active bond management. With a decade of experience managing bonds under my belt, I found myself at the forefront of this evolving landscape, poised to leverage my expertise as the largest sponsor for the rest of my career. I just had to find managers who could handle the assignment.

The traditional 60/40 stock to bond allocation has been a staple in pension investing for quite some time because it provides a balance between growth potential and risk mitigation. I still have the original EAI Asset Allocation presentation book used for an Ivy

League school and a restaurant chain. The manager of EAI's small cap equity fund made the presentation to sell his EAI multi-manager small cap fund as the equity allocation. We suggested an active fixed income account but had no specific selections. I attended but had no part in those asset allocation presentations, nor in any further presentations.

EAI had another fund, a multi-manager hedge fund. Management did not have it in the asset allocation menu. At best, it would be less than 2% allocation with too much oxygen needed to even discuss the product.

My journey with EAI led me to an unexpected opportunity: presenting EAI hedge fund to an EAI client in Salt Lake City. Chad Monroe, EAI's Senior Consultant, orchestrated the chance for me to pitch at one of their quarterly meetings after sensing their potential interest.

This was not just any meeting; it was a chance to pitch our hedge fund to a significant potential customer in the pension industry. The client mandated that all their pension managers and consultants convene in the same room simultaneously, a rarity among pension funds. This arrangement fostered meaningful dialogue centered on investment fundamentals rather than on marketing tactics.

Standing before the gathered executives and the senior portfolio managers of top tier investment firms, I could not help but feel a surge of adrenaline. Chad's confidence in me had led me here, and it was now my responsibility to articulate the value and potential of our hedge fund strategy.

Presenting EAI's hedge fund was an eye-opening experience. With Stanford University's legendary Professor of Finance Jack MacDonald on their board, the investment managers were well-versed in derivatives. His questions sparked lively dialogue among everyone present. However, it became evident that our client might not be ready to invest in a deal arbitrage program at that time.

Nonetheless, the experience offered me a firsthand glimpse into the working of senior pension managers and their board members.

Navigating the world of notoriously secretive hedge fund managers for EAI's alternative fund presented a unique challenge—one that demanded both tact and persistence. Unlike today, there were no voicemails to hide behind; managers answered their own phone. I recall reaching out to Richard 'Scoop' Elden, the founder of Chicago-based Grosvenor Partners, George Weiss of George Weiss Associates of Hartford, Connecticut, and Tom Steyer, founder of Farallon Capital in San Francisco.

When Dick Elden inquired about my EAI Alternatives Group endeavors, I eagerly shared my focus on all-liquid alternatives with a particular emphasis on foreign exchange (FX). Eldon seemed intrigued—this was unlike his usual conversations with EAI Alternatives. My communication with Eldon abruptly ceased. Yet, I received inquiries from management questioning my commitment to liquid alternatives. This puzzling response prompted reflection on my interactions in the hedge fund arena. While Commodity Trading Advisors (CTA's) were responsive and open, other hedge fund entities remained guarded; most reacted strongly to calls during trading time, using aggressive language reminiscent of Wall Street jargon.

The Feshbach brothers, famous for short selling stocks and followers of L. Ron Hubbard, founder of the Church of Scientology, took an unusual approach. Instead of sending hedge fund information, they put me on a Scientology mailing list. Tom Steyer, the billionaire hedge fund manager who ran for President on the Democratic Ticket in 2020, was among those who reacted strongly to calls during trading time.

It was surprising that George Weiss reacted negatively, given our prior acquaintance from my days at Colonial Bank. I took a lot of heat from management for not getting hedge fund information and decided to act like I had at Winchester Western fifteen years earlier.

Knowing George Weiss traded early in the morning, I arrived at his office in Hartford around 3:30 a.m. and knocked on his door. To my surprise, George welcomed me in and invited me to sit next to him on the trading desk. As transactions unfolded, George patiently explained his strategies, ensuring I grasped the intricacies of each move. Despite EAI's lack of enthusiasm for my unconventional approach, I could not have been more satisfied with the outcome. I gained valuable insights that no one else had and rekindled my friendship with George and found him to be a great source of information for me going forward. Despite the challenges, my pursuit of liquid alternatives remained steadfast, fueled by a belief in the potential for innovation and growth in this dynamic field.

I obtained the required hedge fund performance data for Tom Steyer, Farallon Capital and the Feshbach Brothers from David Storrs, President of the Common Fund, a local investment firm in Fairfield, CT, and a client of EAI. David Storrs, a Yale University graduate, preferred Yale graduate investment managers, and I knew he was interested in George Weiss strategies. I called David to mention my time with George on the trading desk where I had observed his strategy execution. During our conversation, I inquired David about his Yale buddy Tom Steyer. David readily provided Tom's performance numbers and asked what else I needed; I mentioned the Feshbach numbers. I drove over to the Common-Fund to pick them up although EAI was displeased as I was not supposed to ask our clients for manager information. Later CommonFund invested a very large amount in George Weiss funds.

The unraveling of the UAL (United Airlines) arbitrage holding within the EAI hedge fund posed a significant problem, particularly given that all three managers had positions in it. Amidst this turbulence, I remained vigilant and continued gathering hedge fund information and performance data while keeping a watchful eye for new investment opportunities for me in Connecticut or New York.

Fortune smiled upon me when the Head of EAI Fixed Income

Research departed the firm. I seized that job as it was a perfect fit for my skills and interests within EAI. Sometimes luck plays a role in career trajectories, and I grabbed the opportunity and never looked back.

Upon transitioning to the role of Head of EAI Fixed Income Research, I found myself immediately tasked by Senior EAI Consultant Chad Monroe to undertake a thorough review of the EAI GIC Manager Research List, 25 Insurance Company Guaranteed Investment Contract (GIC) issuers. EAI received an annual fixed fee for a report on the quality of insurance companies writing GICs.

Chad was aware of my deep-seated concerns regarding the quality of many insurance companies backing Guaranteed Investment Contracts (GICs). My extensive experience as a member of the Investment Group (GPIPC) at MONY, a collective of 44 nationwide insurance investment professionals convening annually, provided valuable insights into this assignment.

At the beginning of the assignment, I tapped into my network of insurance company investment colleagues for help. As I reviewed the EAI GIC Investment list for the first time, I immediately spotted several names that raised red flags. After reaching out to industry contacts, my concerns were validated. Only about half of the listed companies proved to be solid investments.

I reviewed the process with Chad Monroe before communicating our revised 'short list' to the client. Understandably, the client's first reaction was one of dismay, given the drastic changes within a year. However, upon reflection and considering the volatility of credit markets, they came to appreciate the necessity of our actions. Out of transparency, I shared the names of the companies I had contacted. I still have that list of forty-four names today. Given a handful of names and the GIC environment, going forward with an annual review did not make any sense. My first fixed income assignment, and I lost a client.

The reduction of our EAI GIC list surprised consultants, considering the widespread use of GICs as staple in pension benefit plans, 401k, and IRA programs. Traditionally, GICs held a substantial share of fixed income selections. For instance, our initial asset allocation prospect, the Princeton University salaried employees Pension Plan, allocated 35% of its portfolio to GICs.

Organizing an EAI Client Conference required careful consideration, as consultants needed to perceive the agenda as sufficiently compelling to justify their client's attendance at the event, typically held at the Princeton Club in New York City.

With the backing of key figures like Bill Brock, Head of Consulting, and Ellen Petrino, co-founder, along with support of Chad Monroe, I championed a more proactive stance on GICs at EAI. Our efforts culminated in the organization of a client conference at the Princeton Club on March 14, 1991, centered on the theme of 'Alternative GIC Strategies'. This event marked the start of my initiative to transition clients away from GICs toward managed fixed income solutions.

Currency exposure impacts a portfolio's risk in two primary ways: by introducing volatility, which increases risk, and by enhancing diversification, which reduces risk. The dominance of the U.S. bond market, which comprised half of the global fixed income area, sparked an idea. I saw a chance to advocate for diversifying fixed income investments by allocating a portion to international bonds. I believed that by doing so, clients could harness currency diversification to mitigate risk strategically.

The timing could not have been better as external factors aligned in our favor. U.S. Treasury Secretary, Lloyd Bentsen, was pushing for a weaker U.S. dollar, while the German Deutsche Mark surged against it, amid Germany's reunification. I set out to find managers who could leverage this dynamic for investors to take advantage.

Armed with insights from my prior research on liquid alternatives and foreign exchange (FX), I had a supply of data on seasoned international and currency managers. However, convincing clients to incorporate currency exposure into their fixed income portfolios required finesse. Similarly, I framed the discussion around enhancing fixed income allocations without directly highlighting currency exposure. Global bonds sounded less toxic than Non-US, international, or currency exposure.

With the backing again of senior EAI Consultants Ellen Petrino, Chad Monroe and Bill Brock I organized my second EAI Client Conference focused on 'Global Fixed Income' held on November 12, 1991, once again at the Princeton Club. In the six months leading up to the conference, I proactively engaged with experienced international bond managers by inviting them to Norwalk for research and consulting meetings.

I recognized the importance of leveraging the expertise of current experts at handling international bond issues to effectively sell the product. With the assistance of Tony Minopoli, who joined me in fixed income research, we developed EAI's global and international bond databases. Additionally, we crafted comprehensive manager profiles for each manager to be shared with pension clients. This approach ensured that clients should be well-informed and confident in considering global fixed income investments as part of their portfolios.

I frequently utilized the facilities at the Princeton Club whenever I had meetings in NYC. Upon arriving from Connecticut, I got my shoes buffed, freshened up, then went upstairs to the second floor to enjoy a coffee in the spacious room with a fireplace before proceeding out to my meetings. The staff at the Princeton club were familiar with me through my attendance at EAI conferences. Previously, I had been a patron of the Yale Club, located a block away. It was a tradition for me to start and end my NYC visits at the Yale Club with Colonial Banks' Ben Hoffmann a Yale graduate and member. I frequently traveled to NYC with Ben and the Yale staff also became familiar with me.

Consultant Chad Monroe approached me once more with another fixed income project. One of EAI's clients, American Stores, had been employing Western Asset Management as one of their primary fixed income managers. However, Western's performance suffered a setback when a corporate bond issue with a bank defaulted. In response, American Stores requested a meeting with Western Management to address the issue. Surprisingly, instead of sending the portfolio manager, the founder of Western attended the meeting. Unfortunately, he lacked sufficient knowledge about the specific problem, leading American Stores to decide on replacing Western Asset Management.

The EAI consulting team was particularly intrigued by the fixed income bond manager search because there had not been an organized fixed income search in memory. Traditionally, fixed income selections revolved around EAI's Guaranteed Investment Contracts (GIC) list and manager recommendations by pension consultants. Tony Minopoli and I began expanding the EAI bond manager performance databases and crafting manager profiles. Our goal was to create a comprehensive research library solely dedicated to all fixed income managers.

Scheduling meetings with bond managers at EAI's office in Norwalk, Connecticut became a routine, and I ensured to accommodate as many managers as possible throughout the week. Additionally, I recognized the importance of face-to-face interactions and I traveled to New York City at least once a week for meetings with managers based there. Utilizing the convenience of Stratford Airport, I boarded the 'Tube' (a jet with a unique seating arrangement featuring one seat on each side of the aisle, affectionately dubbed the 'flying tube') once a month. After arriving in downtown Boston by 8:30 a.m., I commenced meetings at 9:00 a.m., and returned home on the 4:00 p.m. flight.

Bond managers were eager to meet once they learned about our work on building a manager library and conducting a manager search. With these objectives in mind, I encountered no difficulty in securing meetings.

Drawing on my past experience at an American Stores Board meeting, I structured a list of fixed income candidates for that assignment. Given that American Stores already had PIMCO, I felt it was prudent to diversify with a little less testosterone in fixed income managers. I utilized the Vestek Asset Allocation System program, which was installed on my 20-pound Toshiba laptop with an orange font. Years later, Tony Minopoli complained that the orange font on the Toshiba was probably the reason he needed glasses. Vestek Investment Technology was the state-of-the-art asset allocation technology at that time. I petitioned Bill Brock, Head of EAI Consulting, to help get the software program. Thank you, Bill.

For the American Stores fixed income assignment, I selected three managers: Fred Duda of Harris Investment of Chicago, Karen Coleman of Lowe Brockenbrough Tattersall & Smith of Richmond Virginia, and a third manager whose name I can't recall. Despite their relative anonymity among EAI Consulting staff due to their lack of celebrity status akin to some well-known New York or Boston fixed income managers, I had full confidence in their abilities.

Fred Duda, hailing from Harris Investment in Chicago, was renowned within the industry for his expertise in corporate credits and his conservative investment approach. His stellar track record in navigating the complex mortgage market solidified his reputation. Fred's background as a standout University of Nebraska football player further understored his ability to perform under pressure.

Karen Coleman, representing Lowe Brockenbrough & Tattersall, was highly regarded for her proficiency in structured credit, asset-backed securities, mortgages, and corporate credits. Her impressive track record instilled confidence that she would consistently deliver strong results.

As Chad presented my list of three candidates to American Stores, they were taken aback by the unfamiliar names but agreed to extend invitations to all three for presentations. During Karen Coleman's presentation, an unexpected moment unfolded when Stanford Professor Jack MacDonald, an American Stores Board member, questioned her about her research process with an asset-backed security. When Karen began to quote advice from her professor in response, Jack stood up and interrupted, "You were in my class. I remember you." Karen confirmed this.

In a similar vein, someone at the meeting recalled Fred Duda's football career at Nebraska and his subsequent success going 26-1 as the starting quarterback. All three candidates were hired to replace Western Asset.

Years later, in 2000, during my tenure at Western Asset, Western's CEO, Jim Hirschmann, expressed interest in re-engaging with American Stores. I reached out to Chad at EAI who said, "the three managers that I recommended in 1991 were still there successfully managing American Stores' investments, so probably not a good use of your time. Let me know if you want me to call." There was no call.

My oldest son, Ryan O'Grady, began working at FX Concepts, the world's largest privately owned currency firm, after graduating from Johns Hopkins University. I wanted him to meet some currency managers, so I arranged for him to meet Dave DeRosa, a local Connecticut-based investment research/manager whom I had interviewed and respected in the field of currency management. Dave had recently published a book, titled *Managing Foreign Exchange Risk: Strategies for Global Portfolios* (January 1, 1991), of which he had given me a copy.

A few days before our dinner, I gave Ryan a copy of David's new book. During our dinner, I did not expect Ryan to contribute much to the conversation, and he remained quiet. However, when Dave asked if he looked at the book, Ryan surprised us by pointing out a typo in one of the early chapters relating to an options trade. Dave was taken aback, acknowledging the error but explaining that his publisher was hesitant to reprint or send out a page with the correct equation. Ryan confidently asserted that it was a simple mistake; the signs were reversed.

Although Ryan had not gone through the entire book, he had examined the pages with equations to understand the trades, and he had successfully identified the mistake. This incident highlighted Ryan's aptitude for understanding complex mathematical concepts related to investing and hedging. Over the years, I would call Ryan to ask for help with understanding the math behind investing/hedging concepts.

During our travels for fixed income manager research, Tony Minopoli and I had the opportunity to meet Fred Horton of Dewey Square Advisors in Boston. Our primary objective during these meetings was to identify bond managers capable of enhancing portfolio yield, with a particular emphasis on the new mortgage-backed securities (MBS) introduced by Salomon Brothers' mortgage-backed trading desk.

Salomon Bothers pioneered the practice of pooling home mortgage loans into securities for sale in the bond markets. Spearheaded by Louis Raneri, the Head of Mortgage Trading at Salomon Brothers, this innovative approach played a pivotal role in the early securitization of mortgages. This groundbreaking approach swiftly evolved into a multibillion-dollar industry, transforming the landscape of mortgage financing and fixed income investing.

EAI's focus on mortgaged-backed securities (MBS) in fixed income research presented me with a unique opportunity to serve as the featured luncheon speaker at the Institute for International Research Investing in Mortgage-backed Securities Conference. Held on October 1–2, 1992, at the Parker Meridien Hotel in NYC, this conference brought together industry experts and institutional investors to explore the intricacies of MBS investing.

The theme of my presentation was '*MBS Investing and Pension Funds: The New Wave*', which reflected the growing interest in MBS among institutional investors like pension funds. Following the conference, I distributed copies of my presentation to numerous individuals and organizations.

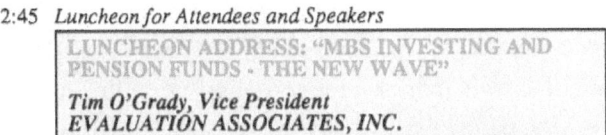

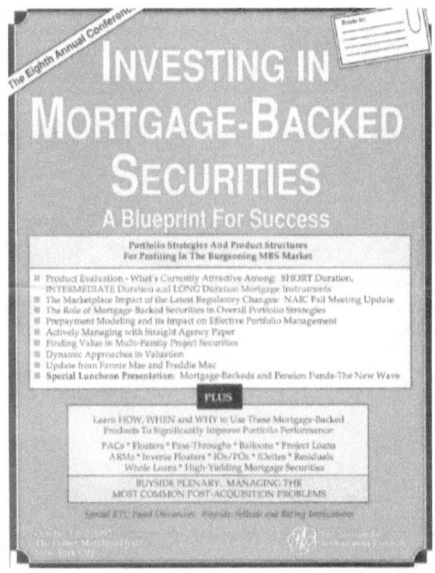

The success of my presentation at the Institute of International Research Investing in Mortgage-Backed Securities Conference opened the door to another speaking opportunity. On October 26, 1992, I received an invitation to join a panel on Strategically Selecting a Fixed Income Manager at the 6th annual Fixed Income

Conference in Miami, Florida. At the conference, I had a chance to observe several global bond managers present and engage with attendees. This experience ultimately contributed to the selection of two global bond managers during my tenure.

I advocated for pension funds to optimize their investment strategies by fully investing their capital, recognizing that a significant portion of their funds was often left idle in cash investments.

My EAI Research fixed income team built a comprehensive list of managers capable of handling short to intermediate duration fixed income products. This initiative marked the first step on the maturity/yield curve ladder of fixed income. Our research recommended transitioning from a monthly cash position to an average maturity of one to three years, thereby maximizing the potential returns on these investments.

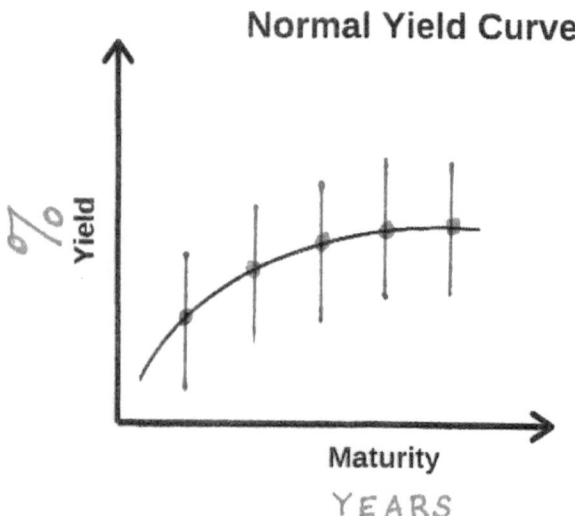

One of my initial recommendations regarding the transition of cash along the yield curve was directed to Hess Oil, which was owned by Leon Hess at the time. Interestingly, Leon Hess also owned the New York Jets football team. Upon arriving at Hess Oil Company in New York for the meeting, I inquired about the location and was directed to the boardroom. Unbeknownst to me, I walked directly into a Hess Oil Board meeting. As I entered and took a seat, I realized the gravity of the situation. I found myself sitting next to EAI consultant John Gardiner, who was visibly embarrassed on my behalf. In a hushed tone, John whispered, "This is a board meeting!" Despite the awkwardness of the situation, Leon Hess continued without acknowledging my presence or interruption.

After the Hess Oil Board meeting, I was introduced to Mr. Hess, who inquired about my family. When I mentioned that I had four sons, he promptly requested some Hess Oil trucks for them. Mr. Hess instructed me to begin with EAI's fixed income manager recommendations, and I started with Neuberger Berman. Mr. Hess expressed familiarity with Roy Neuberger and insisted that Roy attended the meeting when Neuberger was scheduled to present. The formal pension meeting concluded shortly afterward, with Neuberger being the primary topic of discussion.

## 12

## PICKING FIXED INCOME MANAGERS

Following the acquisition of EAI by MONY, the Managers Funds, which were originally part of EAI, transitioned to independence under the ownership of its employees. Despite this change in ownership, EAI Consulting and Research maintained a collaborative relationship with them.

I was asked to review the Managers Funds fixed income manager lineup. The Managers Short & Intermediate Fund had an active duration U.S. Treasury manager. I recommended a change of strategy and manager for the Managers Short & Intermediate Fund. I had been an active duration U.S. Treasury manager during the 1970s at Colonial, but after the Federal Reserve changed operating policy in 1979, I foresaw challenges for the active duration U.S. Treasury strategy. Instead, I advocated for a shift toward a short & intermediate mortgage strategy which not only offered higher yields but also could be managed more efficiently than U.S. Treasuries.

In identifying a suitable manager for this strategy, I believed TCW's Jeff Gundlach stood out as one of the best in the field of mortgage management. Notably, this would mark TCW's first foray into managing a mortgage mutual fund. Although the current fund manager had planned to stay until the end of the month to receive his full fee, Jeff Gundlach agreed to manage the fund for free until the month's end.

A long-term bond fund existed within the Managers Fund and was overseen by the esteemed bond manager Dan Fuss of Loomis Sayles. There had been discussions by The Managers staff to add a mortgage manager to the long-term bond fund. I recommended hiring BlackRock, a relatively new but experienced player in mortgage management. Collaborating closely with one of BlackRock's co-founders, Barbara Novick, I facilitated the process of adding BlackRock to the fund. Notably, this assignment marked BlackRock's inaugural venture into managing a mortgage fund. BlackRock has since ascended to become the world's largest investment manager.

Periodically, I reached out to fixed income giant PIMCO, often speaking with portfolio managers Tad Rivelle or Laird Landman when Bill Gross, the founder, was busy. When Tad & Laird left PIMCO for Hotchkiss & Wiley, I tracked their progress, anticipating an opportunity to observe their presentation skills. When Bill Brock, Head of EAI Consulting, initiated a West Coast search for Griffin Financial Services, I proposed including this new Hotchkiss & Wiley fixed income duo. Though Hotchkiss & Wiley did not win, their presentation impressed everyone. I got a nice letter from Tad & Laird expressing their appreciation. Thank you, Bill Brock, for your trust and support throughout.

In August 1996, Tad & Laird—along with Chris Scibelli, Head of Marketing, and others—decided to establish their own fixed income firm, Metropolitan West. Recognizing the potential of this venture, I flew to Los Angeles to meet with them personally. Throughout the day, we collaborated on creating their Met West fixed income marketing book, to which I contributed insights and suggestions.

Years later, I stumbled upon a signed limited first edition of the

Met West fixed income marketing book and sent it to Chris Scibelli as a gesture of appreciation. Met West became one of the largest fixed income management firms in the world.

One day, I received an SEC subpoena in my mailbox, which led to a visit from the SEC to EAI. During their investigation at Askin Capital's office in New York City, they noted my name on Geoffrey Bradshaw-Mack's calendar. Geoffrey, Askin Capital's Head of Marketing, and a neighbor of mine in Weston, Connecticut would occasionally catch the same Darien train home. Additionally, I frequently reminded him about purchasing tickets for our Kiwanis pancake breakfast fundraiser, which explained the frequent appearance of my name on his calendar. To clarify, I opened my wallet and showed them a Weston Kiwanis pancake breakfast ticket. The SEC got up and left.

Despite thinking my SEC troubles were behind me, my involvement continued when ECAM Funds, the alternative group I had initially worked for, sought my assistance. The alternative group hired Askin Capital as a mortgage manager. I reached out to Geoffrey to arrange a visit to his office to review the portfolio. Although it was a Sunday and the office was closed, we went anyway. Upon arriving at the office, we encountered an Askin portfolio manager going through the portfolio. After an all-day review, the Askin manager determined the portfolio needed a lot of U.S. Treasuries to hedge positions. I was glad he was there because I struggled to grasp the complexities of the mortgage derivative positions in the portfolio.

Months later, I received a second subpoena because I was present in David Askin's office on a Sunday, as reported by the portfolio manager working with Askin. When questioned about my visit, I explained I was there to understand the portfolio composition, relying on the manager's guidance to navigate its complexities. The SEC officials questioned why I would visit if I was not involved with the Askin portfolio. I was trying to help my EAI-alternative friends.

Fifteen years later, while working at Western Asset Management in California, I received a call from lawyers requesting a meeting on Askin. To avoid a subpoena, I flew to New York City for the meeting and underwent questioning. Despite being questioned, I remained silent as I had no connection to Askin. The Bear Stearns lawyer representing the other side viewed my attempt to help with the Askin issue as misguided. He was right!

As previously mentioned, my mom and I have a background with Textron. Textron, an EAI Consulting client, requested a search for a mortgage manager (Remember the mortgage manager that took the pension position that was open when I applied). Textron gave me a list of managers including Billy Williams of STW, a short-term and very long-term fixed income manger. Textron had heard good things about Billy. I expanded the list to include Fred Horton of Dewey Square Advisors, Jeffrey Gundlach of TCW, and Worth Bruntjen of Piper Jaffray, aiming to present Textron with a diverse range of options.

As Dewey Square entered the meeting, they began setting up an easel to display their presentation—a rare sight in a boardroom. However, they encountered difficulties as the stand kept falling over. Since time was precious, Fred gave the presentation from their book.

Jeff Gundlach's presentation at TCW left a lasting impression on everyone present, including the Textron team. He made a bold entrance by passing out his mortgage book and instructing everyone not to open it, declaring that he would explain everything himself. Throughout the 45-minute presentation, Jeff captivated the audience with insights into his approach to portfolio construction.

There was not a single comment during or after the presentation—just stunned silence. While I do not recall if TCW ultimately secured a portion of the portfolio, I do remember that Worth Bruntjen won the assignment. During his presentation, Worth focused on correcting the previous manager's mistakes, leveraging his expertise and familiarity with the existing portfolio which I had not seen. The discussion also veered into topics like breeding and racing horses, which some of the Textron board members and Worth were involved with.

Soon after, Worth got caught by the same rapidly rising interest rates in early 1994. The resulting decline in performance prompted Textron to transition from Worth to TCW. Prior to this move, I reached out to TCW to ensure they were prepared and could act swiftly. TCW's new mortgage portfolio manager, Fred Horton (sans easel this time), stepped in to address the situation. EAI's cofounder Ellen Petrino and I advocated for TCW to hire Fred Horton when Fred decided he needed a change.

Fred took charge of the Textron portfolio and implemented the necessary changes, receiving praise from Textron. Meanwhile, TCW also assumed responsibility for Worth Bruntjen's mortgage portfolio from the State of New Hampshire, with Jeffrey Gundlach overseeing the portfolio pro bono until arrangements could be finalized. It is worth noting that the Jeffrey Gundlach whom you see on TV is not the same Jeffrey I worked with during my tenure.

Mike Randazzo took over from Tony Minopoli who had been promoted to work under Chad Monroe as a Consultant Associate. Mike joined our team, initially working alongside Tony and me as we prepared for Tony's transition. Mike brought a wealth of experience, as he had been an outstanding baseball player (he served as the captain of the Seaton Hall baseball team and played a key role in their victory as the 2001 Big East Baseball Champions). Additionally, Mike had a brief stint playing professional baseball for the Chicago White Sox.

With Mike and Tony's help, I became an EAI Partner on February 1, 1994. Up to that point, I had given seven speeches, not only in New York but also in places like West Virginia and Toronto.

One of my notable speeches was in West Virginia on June 21, 1993, titled 'Mortgage-Backed Securities, Safety, Stability and Superior Return'. I gave this speech just two days after I underwent chest surgery to remove a growth. I was not supposed to travel. I was still a little lightheaded, which probably killed any anxiety.

I really worked hard for my partnership and although I did not generate revenue, I supported consultants in their efforts. I was looking forward to my ownership but was offered only ½ %. A ½% ownership was a big disappointment.

# 13

## THE O'GRADY FAMILY MOVES TO WESTON

The decision to relocate my family from Watertown to Weston was necessary to reduce the logistical challenges of commuting to my job in Norwalk. The lack of a direct main route made the daily commute cumbersome. I continued commuting until my oldest son Ryan graduated from Taft High School. Interestingly, Ryan never lived with us in Weston. At sixteen years old, he went straight to Johns Hopkins University in Baltimore, Maryland.

Our decision to settle in Weston was primarily influenced by the quality of the schools and the renowned high school swimming and diving program. During that period, Greenwich (LL), Wilton (L), and Weston (M) boasted some of the best high school swimming and diving programs in Connecticut. My son Jamie had already made a mark in diving, lettering at Watertown High as a freshman when Watertown High beat heavyweight Naugatuck High for the Naugatuck Valley League-NVL Swim Championship.

Weston is a town north of Westport, Connecticut in Fairfield County. Emmy and Academy award actor and Weston resident Christopher Plummer best describes Weston, Connecticut: "There are no streetlights, no town water, no sewers, no industry, no condominiums, no automobile dealers, no franchises, no movie theaters and, we don't even have sidewalks. In fact, come to think of it, we don't have much of anything, and most of us want to keep it that way."

Many Connecticut and NYC executives lived in town and did not care what it cost in taxes to have a great school complex. Just driving through town, you could smell the wealth. If you looked at Weston through Google Maps, all you would see were a canopy of treetops. If you zoomed in closer, you could see the Weston School complex.

We purchased a new manufactured home in the heart of Weston, Connecticut, strategically located near the schools for our boys' convenience. Both Lorraine and I maintained full-time jobs, so our evenings and weekends were dedicated to transforming our home. Nestled amidst the woods on Weston Road, our residence initially appeared overgrown and neglected. However, with the help of our neighbor Charlie McCullough, who generously shared his tools and expertise, we embarked on a year-long journey to renovate and landscape our property to perfection. My dedication to yard work earned me the affectionate title of 'Weston Maintenance', immortalized on a red sweatshirt crafted by my wife. However, the constant interruptions from passersby seeking yard work eventually promptly to retire the sweatshirt. (See Appendix for a photo of the shirt)

The move was tough on my family. We left behind the comfort of a spacious home, a close-knit neighborhood, and top-tier schools. My role at Colonial Bank also provided a sense of stability and prominence. In Weston, however, our lifestyle underwent a noticeable shift. My kids did not have the latest bikes and our vacations became more modest, foregoing extravagant trips to Europe or skiing in Lake Tahoe.

My son Jamie, a sophomore at Weston High, joined the high

school swim team as a diver. Living next door to Ralph Rynning, Weston's top diver, provided him with inspiration and guidance. Although the Weston swim team started the season slowly, they gained momentum, and went on to win another Class M Championship. Jamie's dedication and skill earned him a spot at Connecticut's All-States Diving Championships at Yale's Payne Whitney Gymnasium. During the first day's dives, only eight divers advanced to the second round, and Jamie was among them.

During the second day, Jamie and Ralph found themselves discussing the dives they were required to complete. It became apparent that Jamie was self-taught, as Weston High lacked a diving coach. Despite this, Jamie performed admirably, securing fifth place in dives he only attempted once.

It took several years before my other two sons felt comfortable, made friends, and fit in. If I had known how awful it was going to be for them, I would have continued to commute from Watertown, Connecticut.

I became a member of the Kiwanis Club of Weston, a diverse group consisting of firefighters, local and state representatives, corporate executives, and small business owners. Our Saturday morning meetings, held for breakfast at a local church, accommodated members who still worked. Lorraine encouraged me to join as we have always been involved in community activities wherever we lived, and we wanted our four sons to participate as well. Volunteering became a family affair, and I found immense satisfaction in the work.

In March 1993, Lorraine and made the decision to host a Saint Patrick's Party at our new home in the Singing Oaks complex. This property had once been a day camp managed by Peter Meehan and his wife Rhee. Our home sat on 3.25 acres of land and served as the model house for the development, as it was meticulously designed to showcase the builder's craftsmanship.

Victor Niederhofer, our only immediate neighbor, lived in

Weston's largest home a 25,000 square foot mansion within a gated complex. Victor often strolled past our home and would pause to watch my sons playing roller hockey on our newly paved road.

Months after our Saint Patrick's party, Victor Niederhofer graciously invited my family for dinner and a special Broadway play performance. Victor went all out for the occasion and arranged for the cast of a Broadway play to be transported to his home in Weston. He created an intimate theater experience for his guests by setting up a stage in his spacious living room.

As my family lined up in the kitchen for food, I couldn't help but overhear Victor engaging in conversation with members of George Soros' hedge fund trading team. It was intriguing to learn that Victor had collaborated with Soros for about a decade before venturing out on his own. The Soros team praised Victor's remarkable track record in the hedge fund industry, citing consistent gains of 30% compounded over twenty years. George Soros himself was not present for dinner, but the conversation provided valuable insights, and we thoroughly enjoyed the Broadway play that followed. This encounter also facilitated the establishment of several connections within Soros' hedge fund network.

During my tenure as President of Kiwanis, I enlisted the help of Harvey Shapiro, a senior executive at SONY, to organize our annual spring pancake breakfast fundraiser. Harvey had an illustrious career at Columbia Records, where he showcased his talent for discovering new singing sensations, including the likes of Michael Bolton. Even after SONY acquired Columbia Records, Harvey remained a key figure in the music industry.

Our fundraising efforts exceeded all expectations under Harvey's leadership. The initial modest fundraising goal of $1500 ballooned into an astonishing net income of over $7,000—remarkable success when tickets cost $3.00.

In recognition of our achievement, Harvey graciously invited my family to join him for lunch at SONY Corporation of America

Headquarters in New York City. Despite his senior position, Harvey was known for his casual attire, standing out among the suited executives at SONY. His warm personality attracted attention wherever he went, and many colleagues stopped by to greet him during our visit.

After a delightful lunch in the executive suite, Harvey gave us an exclusive tour of SONY recording studios. We had the privilege of witnessing Mariah Carey in action, as she was recording her latest tracts. At that time, Mariah Carey was married to Tommy Mottola, the influential President of SONY Music Entertainment.

A few years later, as homes on Singing Oaks Drive began to take shape, Victor Niederhoffer extended an invitation to his neighbors for a barbeque at his residence. Victor graciously welcomed us into his home, where he gave us a personal tour of his impressive silver and memorabilia collections. One of the highlights of the tour was Victor's home squash court, a unique feature nestled within the confines of his residence. During our visit, my son Jamie had the opportunity to play a friendly game of squash with Victor. (Victor was National Champion in 1966 and in the years 1972–1975; National Doubles Champion in 1968, 1973, and 1974; and North American Open Champion in 1975.) The picture shows Victor and me on his lawn. Victor was very interested in my fixed income trading skills.

Living near our church, Emmanuel Episcopal Church, the blind musician and singer Jose Feliciano, renowned for his songs 'Light My Fire' and 'Feliz Navidad', was a notable neighbor. Each Sunday, we would pass by Jose's residence on our way to and from church.

One Sunday, one of my sons suggested inviting Jose to join the Kiwanis Club or to attend one of our fundraisers. Intrigued, I extended an invitation to Jose to join our Kiwanis Club.

To formalize the invitation, my mother-in-law, Agnes Phillips, who possessed a braille typewriter and used it to assist individuals in

Ridgefield Park, New Jersey, volunteered to compose a braille letter inviting Jose to a Kiwanis meeting. Agnes crafted the invitation, and we mailed it to Jose.

During one of his radio programs, Jose mentioned receiving the invitation from the Kiwanis Club. He expressed gratitude but due to his commitments, including his preparing for his radio show on Saturdays and his demanding travel schedule, he regretfully declined the invitation to join.

Despite living in the same town as notables like Keith Richards, Robert Redford, or Christopher Plummer, I never sent them breakfast invitations. However, I considered extending an invitation to Christopher Walken, who resides in nearby Wilton, Ct. One day while driving to work, I passed Christopher Walken walking or jogging along Weston Road. It took me a moment to recognize him. When I turned the car around to approach him, he had already vanished. I can only imagine he recognized my license plate, OGRADY, and decided to avoid any potential sales pitches by making a quick exit. Yes, this is the same Christopher Walken that was just on one of the Super bowl commercials.

## 14

## PICTURES UP

Converting outdated equity profile requirements into a fixed income manager profile for our research library was a project I had been mulling over for some time. Updating manager profiles was not in the EAI IT budget, but I saw the need and potential value in making this change.

A neighbor of mine in Weston had an interesting role in producing credit card commercials for television. What intrigued me was that his name appeared on the credit card in the commercial. When I inquired about how he managed to do this, he simply replied that it was easy—he was the boss. This interaction sparked an idea in my mind about filming investment manager meetings at EAI.

Having previously filmed myself practicing the Protected Equity/Portfolio Insurance presentation for the entire staff at MONY, I recognized the power of utilizing film for research and potential marketing purposes. Each conversation with my neighbor fueled my imagination and sparked ideas about how to integrate film into my manager research work.

Typically, portfolio manager meetings or research sessions

adhere to a scripted format within a one-hour timeframe. However, often a significant portion of this time, around fifteen minutes, is eaten up by introductions, seating arrangements, and the distribution of presentation materials. By filming these meetings, I envisioned cutting down on wasted time and creating a more focused review, ultimately resulting in a more efficient use of everyone's time.

Recognizing the value of thorough documentation, I began crafting a script of questions for managers, which ensured that we covered all relevant topics during our discussions. One particular beneficial aspect of having a script was addressing performance issues. By recording managers' responses, we could later compare their statements to actual outcomes.

My vision was to develop a robust film library accessible to our research or consultant teams in order to provide them with a resource to reference whenever they had inquiries about an investment manager or a particular strategy. I drew inspiration from pioneering efforts like the California Public Employees' Retirement System. They had already begun filming manager presentations for their investment manager searches.

In November 1994, I embarked on a bold mission to research global bond and currency managers in London, England, known as the world's currency center. Despite never having been to London and lacking any connections in the city, I decided to film my investment manager visits for EAI consultants back home. Equipped with nothing but my trusty family video camera—a bulky 1970s VHS recorder resembling a small bazooka—I set out to capture the essence of London's bond and currency managers.

My goal was to provide EAI consultants with a firsthand glimpse into how London managers presented themselves and their strategies. I had concerns that some English global bond managers might come across as stiff and overly conservative, which might not align with preferences of EAI's mostly East Coast mid-sized corporate pension clients. In my view, bond managers needed to be more than just knowledgeable; they needed to be engaging storytellers who could articulate complex market issues and currency dealings in a compelling manner.

To maximize my time in London, I reached out to EAI consultants for recommendations on firms and portfolio managers to meet. With a combined list of eighteen manager meetings lined up, I faced the challenge of squeezing them into four and a half days. This meant scheduling four one-hour meetings per day across the sprawling city of London.

I planned my itinerary to solve this logistical puzzle, ordering London street maps and spending weeks arranging manager schedules based on their locations' zip codes. Navigating the city efficiently was key, so I relied on London cabbies to get me from one meeting to another.

Despite a missed opportunity to connect during their visit to New York a few months prior, Paribas Global expressed interest in meeting with me. As they were a new player in the U.S. pension investor market with numerous questions, I agreed to meet them at their office on Sunday afternoon, marking it as 'meeting #19' on my calendar. Given the informal nature of the meeting, I opted not to bring along my trusty camera.

The meeting with Paribas was successful for both parties. I provided them with valuable insights on which pension consultants would align with their strategies, and also shared my list of eighteen recommended manager calls. In return, they offered valuable background information on managers they admired and explained why, which proved to be a great coup for me ahead of my other meetings.

In 2010, Olaf Rogge of Rogge Global Partners, one of EAI recommended global bond managers, and I were in the movies. I had a part in *Iron Man 2* with Robert Downey Jr., and Olaf was a consultant with a speaking part in Wall Street movie *Money Never*

*Sleeps,* better known as *Wall Street 2*. We agreed to get together in London to have a cocktail to celebrate. We have yet to do that.

When I walked into my first manager meeting early on Monday morning, I was led into a conference room where I set up my trusty video/bazooka and started recording as soon as employees arrived in the room. With each employee's entrance, I found myself recording and perhaps unintentionally capturing most of the firm's staff who wandered in to see what I was doing. The situation was far from what I had expected. Nobody was quite sure how to react to the unexpected filming. I had reminded the manager beforehand that I would be filming our meetings and giving them a heads-up about the presence of the camera. To break the ice, I jokingly suggested that everyone should "pretend I am from CNN."

Almost immediately, I realized that I had picked the wrong firm to start filming. This firm was not even on my original list of eighteen managers; no one had requested them, and they had not sent over the materials that I had requested before my London trip. Their office happened to be conveniently located next to my hotel —an opportunistic but ultimately questionable choice.

I did not know how disruptive using a video camera was for manager interviews. Many senior managers came across as stiff, conservative, and reserved—just name rank and serial number. They were uncomfortable with filming because client records, client portfolios, and trading positions were open on desktops.

As the week progressed, my filming technique improved, and I grew more comfortable with the process. By Tuesday afternoon, word had spread among the managers on my visit list about the camera, prompting some to call others in anticipation of my arrival.

During one incident, the Head of Investments at JP Morgan Investment Management (JPMIM) contacted Victor Filatov of Smith Barney to inform him of my delayed arrival and JP Morgan's request for an extended meeting duration. The JPMIM executive ensured that I did not try to film their trading room.

Although I did not film near the JP Morgan trading desk, I did capture footage at Warburg's offices, as directed by Rory Macleod. Rory had me film the dealers and their direct lines with Central Banks, as well as a dealer executing currency and bond trades on a broker screen.

Upon my return to the EAI office, the first question I received was whether I had tea at 3:00 p.m. at Rothschild, which indeed I did, albeit unintentionally. Despite being late for several meetings, the timing allowed for a formal tea experience.

Ultimately, I chose not to showcase the film to EAI Consultants, as they preferred verbal communication about the managers and meetings. Once EAI Research established a global bond buy list, inquiries focused more on complex investment strategies, where verbal communication proved more effective than visual aids. I found the London film to be a valuable resource for insights into back-office operations and procedures that I would not typically glean from manager visits at EAI in Norwalk, CT. Additionally, it allowed me to make connections with traders during evening gatherings for cocktails, further expanding my global network.

Traders proved to be eager conversationalists and provided me with valuable insights and gossip from the London scene. Recognizing the importance of continuous learning, I made it a priority to return to London whenever possible.

I made one final attempt as a fixed income film producer, I extended an invitation to Jack Sommers, co-founder, and portfolio manager at Income Research & Management (IR&M) in Boston to address EAI's Fixed Income Research and consultants about Corporate Put Bonds. Put bonds held a key focus of IR&M, a relatively new fixed income firm founded by a father-son duo, John and Jack Sommers.

This event marked the first instance where I focused on a father and son investment team, a theme that would later resonate deeply with me when I joined my son Ryan O'Grady's firm, ROW Asset

Management, in 2012. Jack Sommers did an excellent job in front of a packed room. I still have the film of the presentation.

Despite my continued offers to produce research films, there was minimal interest. Instead, consultants would reach out to me if they were interested in particular strategy or a manager.

## 15

## TAKING THE MESSAGE TO THE PEOPLE

I remained committed to participating in speaking engagements in New York City, aiming to elevate awareness of EAI's Fixed Income Research among pension prospects. Given EAI Consulting's focus on mid-size corporate clients on the east coast, I prioritized these engagements to ensure maximum outreach in this important market. Additionally, I made sure to be available and known to sponsors whenever London hosted a fixed income or currency conference. I was very proactive to seize any opportunity to showcase EAI's expertise and capabilities in the global financial markets

In Chicago, I had the honor of kicking off the conference as the first speaker on day one. I began my presentation with slide that instantly caught everyone's attention: 'Currency Counts'. Jeffrey Geller, Head of Currency Management at BEA and a fellow speaker, commended the effectiveness of this opening slide in capturing the audience's interest and setting the tone for discussions ahead.

After the success of the conferences in NYC and Chicago, a third Foreign Exchange Conference with the theme Currency Risk Control Strategies for Global Portfolios was scheduled for October

2, 1995, in London. I eagerly accepted the opportunity to return to London and present alongside the best global currency managers and consultants based in the city. Additionally, I assured my EAI bosses that I would utilize my time in London to meet with potential managers.

During the conference, my panel was assigned the last slot in the afternoon agenda. Drawing inspiration from the practice of heavyweight manager PIMCO who preferred to go last in presentations, I decided to request the same for myself. As I began my presentation, the overhead slide screen bulb unexpectedly blew out. Without missing a beat, I improvised by lifting the slide, collecting all my slides, and proceeding to walk around the room, presenting and changing slides as I went. This impromptu approach received a round of applause from the audience. My son, Ryan O'Grady, who was working at FX Concepts in NYC, heard about the incident where "the guy walked around with the slides after the lights went out."

Immediately after the conference concluded, Michael Huffman of Millennium Global Investments approached me to discuss his global bond portfolio. Despite previous attempts to connect with Michael regarding his currency overlay team and global bond management program, we had been unable to coordinate. Now Michael expressed an interest in showcasing his portfolio that was set inside the JP Morgan Risk Metrics variance model.

Having been familiar with JP Morgan's Risk Metrics program, I was intrigued to see its impact on global fixed income investment portfolios. Michael, who had previously worked at JP Morgan and spearheaded their currency overlay business, took time to walk me through the intricacies of the risk management system.

I secured a meeting with Liaquat Ahamed, the Chief Investment Officer at Fischer Francis Trees and Watts (FFT&W), to understand their portfolio strategy against the Lehman Global Aggregate Index. Liaquat explained their process meticulously, including their adjustments of bond exposures and durations for each country as well as currency, even for currencies not in the benchmark. This confirmed FFT&W as a key global bond manager for EAI Research.

Upon returning from London, I realized the necessity of acquiring technology to enhance my understanding of risk in global portfolios. Throughout my career—whether at Colonial Trust, Colonial Bank, Roosevelt & Cross, MONY and now EAI Consulting—I consistently advocated for access to the latest technology available.

I ended 1995 as the luncheon speaker at the Boston Security Analysts Society 'Currency Policy Issues' as my presentation topic. I thanked Scudder's Global Bond Portfolio Manager Mark Turner, and Mark Kritzman, owner of Windham Capital, for their assistance in securing this prestigious invitation.

During my discussion with Mark Kritzman, I learned about his software development aimed at estimating the risk and diversification properties of a portfolio's currency. Recognizing the potential of this tool, I recalled a strategy used years prior with Gifford Fong when acquiring his software for portfolio insurance. Inspired by this, I approached Mark Kritzman and requested a discounted lease for his software. Fortunately, Mark agreed to my proposal.

Instead of solely relying on a portfolio's actual exposures, the program utilized historical exposure data from relevant market indices as a proxy for currency exposure. Each country's currency was the primary hedge, but more liquid, correlated currencies were used when available to reduce costs. EAI Fixed Income Research adopted eleven primary hedge currencies, four of which (Deutsche Mark, Japanese Yen, Great Britain Pound, and U.S. dollar) also served as basket hedges. Using the Kritzman optimizer, we could decide if any of these currencies should be sold short to effectively hedge the underlying exposure, enhance risk-return strategies.

On February 1, 1996, EAI Research, led by Timothy J.

O'Grady and Janice B. Naarden in collaboration with Steven Peplowski, Associate Consultant published a white paper, titled *Developing a Currency Hedge Ratio*. The paper explored currency hedging strategies and offered valuable insights into the development of effective hedge ratios. The significance of the white paper was underscored when it was picked up by the Journal of Pension Investing, edited by Joelyn Flomenhaft. Due to its publication in Volume 2.2, in the Fall of 1977, it reached a wider audience than just EAI consultant clients.

From 1991 to 1999, I delivered a total of thirty-four speeches across seven states and three countries, covering various topics related to investment portfolios and risk management. Additionally, I authored five white papers during this period. One notable speech, titled 'Currency Risk in Investment Portfolios', presented at the AIMR Conference, was published in June 1999.

I was following the progress of the European Monetary Union (EMU). Stage three was scheduled to begin on June 1, 1999, where the national currencies of eleven European countries—Austria, Belgium, Finland, France, Germany, Ireland, Italy, Luxembourg, the Netherlands, Portugal, and Spain—were unified into a single currency, the Euro.

Simultaneously, I began my year-long work delving into my family genealogy tracing our roots back to Athenry, County Galway. My primary objective was to obtain my grandfather Peter O'Grady's birth certificate which I needed to prove my Irish heritage to qualify for dual citizenship and acquire an Irish EU passport. The Irish EU passport facilitated my research visits to European countries.

I successfully persuaded EAI Management to organize an EAI Client Conference, titled 'Countdown to EMU: European Monetary Union'. I advocated for this conference because I believed it was crucial for our clients to comprehend that eleven European currencies would cease to exist on January 1, 1999, to be replaced by the Euro. During the 1990s, global and international bond managers capitalized on buying several 'weaker' European currencies while shorting the strong German Deutsche Mark. The expectation was that the value of weaker currencies would appreciate as they merged into the strong Euro. Anticipating that the Euro would emerge as a competitor to the U.S. dollar, I wanted to ensure that U.S. investors we well-informed about upcoming changes.

In preparation for a panel discussion on the European Monetary Union (EMU) and the introduction of the Euro currency, I invited four esteemed global bond managers to join the discussion. From left to right, the panelists were London-based Rory MacLeod, Chief Investment Officer at Barclays Bank; Lee Thomas, Managing Director at PIMCO; Ray Dalio, founder of Bridgewater Associates and London-based Morgan Stanley, Chief Investment Officer David Germany.

The panel did an excellent job elucidating the rationale behind the transition to a single European currency and the establishment of a unified European trading bloc to bolster competitiveness vis-à-vis the USA and China.

The passing of Major League Baseball Umpire Gerry McSherry during the opening game of the 1996 Major League Baseball season in Cincinnati on April 1 brought about an unexpected challenge for EAI Consulting. As a client of Major League Baseball, EAI became involved when PIMCO's co-founder and Senior Portfolio Manager Bill Gross published a monthly investment letter, 'Investment

Outlook', in which he compared the umpire's weight excesses and subsequent death to the state of the U.S. economy.

Linda Schissel, EAI's Senior Consultant managing the Major League Baseball account, sought assistance in addressing the situation. Despite initial resistance from PIMCO attributed to Bill Gross's editorial autonomy over his topics, efforts were made to address the issue. To facilitate this, I reached out to Tom Kendal and Ronnie Di Pasquale from Wasserstein Perella Asset Management, as they had connections to PIMCO through their former boss at Salomon Brothers, William Thompson Jr., who was now PIMCO's CEO and Bill Gross's superior.

I did not have high expectations until Tom Kendall called back to confirm a meeting scheduled by William Thompson Jr. in the late afternoon after market hours. After arranging my trip, I arrived at PIMCO, feeling nervous about the meeting. Many PIMCO staff members approached me, curious about my connection to William Thompson Jr. I improvised and claimed we were old friends. In William's office, we spoke briefly before joining a conference room where Bill Gross, Brent Harris, Doug Hodge, and John Hague were present.

William Thompson Jr. outlined the purpose of the meeting regarding client concerns over one of PIMCO's Investment Outlook letters, and then tasked me to address the situation with Major League Baseball. During discussions with Bill Gross, we exchanged views on the appropriateness of the comments. While he acknowledged the concerns, Bill Gross asserted his editorial license. After our discussion, he left, and I returned to William Thompson's office, where he thanked me for confronting Bill Gross. Although there were no immediate changes, the encounter signaled to EAI consultants would assert themselves. Eventually, the Major League Baseball account left PIMCO. While I did not view it as a victory, EAI valued the opportunity for direct dialogue with PIMCO's CEO and Bill Gross.

Two decades later, my son James O'Grady, who has his own investment firm—Braemar Wealth Management, an LPL firm—attended a Janus presentation featuring Bill Gross, Janus' new fixed income manager. Remembering my encounter with Bill Gross regarding the Major League Baseball umpires incident, I suggested to Jamie to say 'hello' to Bill Gross and mention my tenure at EAI and the Major League Baseball Umpires meeting with him. Jamie went right up to Bill Gross after the presentation and told him his dad had worked for EAI and met him to talk about the umpire passing. Surprisingly, Bill Gross remembered me and discussed the meeting with Jamie. Then they had a picture taken with together.

I was so lucky at EAI to have young partners like Tony Minopoli, Mike Randazzo, Janice Naardin, John Cardinali, and Alec Rapaport working with me during my EAI career. They grew up with technology and stepped right in to help develop EAI research. As my career expanded, my young partners had a chance to grow with me. Alec Rapaport helped with fixed income and international equity when I took over that assignment. He and I travelled together to Hong Kong and Tokyo to interview both global equity and bond managers. Our flight to Hong Kong left JFK with a stop in Los Angeles, then on to Kai Tak (the old Hong Kong airport). I noticed our flight to Hong Kong was not over water but over land because of serious storms in the Pacific Ocean. Our flight back home from Tokyo never got off the ground. As we were preparing for takeoff, the right-side jet engine had flames. The flames died. Then a guy with a pickup truck and a large wrench came up and started hitting the inside of the engine. That caused panic in the airplane, and we disembarked. Our passports were taken, and we were bused to an airport hotel before flying home on a new plane the following day.

I worked with the consultants trying to solve fixed income and equity (stock) problems. A unique challenge arose when Colgate Palmolive sought counsel on hedging their equity investments, a task typically outside the purview of fixed income specialists like me. Collaborating with colleagues such as Tony Minopoli and Ed Filusch, Vice President & Treasurer at Colgate, we proposed a temporary hedging strategy involving S&P 500 equity index futures to mitigate risk and capture alpha. The proposal, eventually brought before Colgate's Board, highlighted the absence of alpha in their current equity management. This revelation, however, elicited unexpected reactions from one equity manager who could not fathom how a 'bond person' could influence their domain.

I collaborated Phil Nehro, Executive Vice President of Alliance Capital Management Global Derivatives, on a bond hedging proposal for Colgate. Phil's expertise and guidance were instrumental as we delved into the intricacies of a ten-year treasury total return swap spanning a three-year period. Phil worked with Tony and me on the presentation book which Chad Monroe presented to Colgate. While Colgate expressed interest, they sought validation from their derivative consultant, Phil Nehro. Phil reviewed the presentation and provided guidance to Colgate, unbeknownst to them that he had already collaborated with us on the proposal. During a break, Phil called me, really upset. I could never tell him who the client was. Phil said if he had known who the client was, it would have been a much shorter exercise for him. Our collaboration with Phil elevated EAI Fixed Income Research within the consulting community. The Colgate derivative consultant did not change anything in our presentation!

# 16

# WESTERN ASSET MANAGEMENT COMPANY

Despite being neighbors in southern Connecticut, our paths had not crossed prior to recruitment by Western. Ken Leach, Western's CIO, worked with Al McClymonds at Credit Suisse First Boston in NYC. Recognizing Al's expertise and success in hedge fund management, Ken saw him as an ideal fit for the new hedge fund assignment given his robust Wall Street background.

Before joining Western Asset in June 1999, Al McClymonds and I met to outline securities and strategies for a fixed income relative value hedge fund, expanding beyond the cash-futures treasury basis trade. Al suggested involving Jai Choi, Western Asset's mortgage/swaps manager who brought valuable experience from Goldman Sachs. It was clear we needed to establish a structure and hire employees to develop risk monitoring and reporting systems, with input from Compliance.

In May 1999, I attended a meeting at Deutsche Bank in NYC to discuss initiating a high-yield CDO program at Western. Unfortunately, the meeting did not lead to any progress due to the lack of required seed capital from either party. Western's owner, Legg Mason, had no intention of seeding a family of CDOs, hedge funds, or any other alternative programs. I chose not to share this setback with my wife, as it might have influenced her decision to move to California.

I moved to California in June 1999 with five suitcases. It was not a trial run. I was committed to building fixed income products. Lorraine stayed behind in Connecticut to handle the packing and moving logistics.

A high-yield CDO program was essential when I arrived. Months before joining, my partner at EAI, Alec Rapaport, prepared presentations for me on high-yield and asset-backed CDOs. I used these during the initial CDO presentation to Western's Client Service team to familiarize them with the product and address their questions.

However, Western's high-yield managers were hesitant to oversee a private placement leveraged product. As a result, the project was paused until I could find a portfolio manager within Western willing to oversee such an asset class. In the interim, I redirected my efforts toward securing seed capital for hedge funds and starting a TIPs fund.

During my tenure at EAI, I attended meetings at the U.S. Treasury in New York City as a guest of Bridgewater. These meetings provided valuable insights into the development and launch of U.S. Treasury Inflation Protected Securities (TIPS). TIPS differ significantly from conventional Treasuries because they adjust their principal monthly based on the Consumer Price index (CPI). This adjustment protects against inflation, ensuring the principal increases with the inflation rate and providing a real rate of interest. Due to their unique features, TIPS were often misunderstood by traders and buyers, leading to their cheap pricing at auction. I saw an opportunity in trading these liquid yet misunderstood securities.

Even before joining Western, I had been envisioning a series of TIPS products. My proposal included launching two TIPS funds: a standard mutual fund and a levered TIPS fund. The primary focus was on the TIPS mutual fund, which required no seed capital.

Scott Mullet spearheaded the initiative, collaborating closely with lawyer Brian Chegwidden from Ropes & Gray, Western Asset Legal and economist Scott Grannis. The project garnered support, with several Western portfolio managers volunteering to manage the mutual fund as soon as we announced it.

Randy Kohn, Al McClymonds, and I successfully convinced Western's Client Service Executive/Marketing Group to seed a levered U.S. TIPS hedge fund. With $2 million in seed capital—future bonus payments—from our group and contributions from some portfolio managers, we launched the WA Inflation Linked Opportunity Fund.

A few of our Wall Street brokers friends suggested that Al McClymonds and I schedule meetings with The Hartford and Aetna Insurance Companies, believing they were interested in a levered TIPS program. However, just before our scheduled meetings, Western Asset's Jay Choi advised us to cancel, as both companies were already developing similar products. Despite this setback, we had productive discussions with prime brokers like Bear Stearns and Merrill Lynch in New York about financing for our levered TIPS positions.

The Merrill financing representative initially struggled to grasp the concept of TIPS. Al McClymonds clarified that TIPS principal increases monthly based on the inflation rate (CPI), and Western would sell some of the principal to cover financing costs. Eventually, the representative understood.

However, our levered TIPS effort faced a setback when Legg Mason halted additional funding from Western employees. Legg expressed discomfort with the idea of Western offering an alternative fund exclusively to a select number of Pasadena trading and marketing employees.

The levered TIPS Fund persevered and remained operational despite challenges. By January 2000, expanded credit guidelines made its track record more marketable. A Confidential Offering Memorandum for Western Asset Opportunistic Value Portfolio N.V. (account number 1074) was prepared on August 22, 2001. The fund remained operational when I left in March of 2009.

Despite obstacles in marketing a TIPS fund in alternative space, progress on the TIPS mutual fund initiative continued. On March 1, 2001, the Western Asset Inflation Indexed Plus Bond mutual fund was successfully launched.

Scott Mullet joined me after the departure of Curt Livingston, Western Asset's founder, CEO, CIO. Curt's exit was surprising given our discussions regarding my role at Western while I was at EAI. Curt was keen on understanding competitors' strategies and aligning them with Western's goals. We had numerous discussions on integrating global bond assignments and emerging market debt into Western's domestic fixed income approach, which Curt was exploring.

During my time at EAI, General Electric (GE) worked on a program to consolidate all pension investments under a single management firm. This move combined indexed and actively managed strategies with the aim of streamlining reporting, cutting costs, improving efficiency, and potentially boosting returns across the pension portfolio. This approach mirrored an industry trend toward optimization for better outcomes for pension funds.

Western Asset was excluded from GE's manager search program due to a lack of equity and international management. Curt asked me to compare a Legg Mason Family product using Legg Mason for equity, Western Asset for domestic fixed income, and Brandywine for global bonds. Using an optimizer, I combined the returns, consistently matching or surpassing those of single-manager firms. Despite this, Legg Mason was not included in the final selection due to the absence of a centralized asset allocator. I suggested to Curt that he invite Brandywines' global bond managers to Pasadena to explore synergies. Despite a meeting, no concrete developments emerged.

In 1994, Keith Gardner transitioned to Western Asset from Legg Mason to lead its Emerging Market Debt program. Additionally, in December 1995, Legg Mason acquired London based Lehman Brothers Global Asset Management and renamed it 'Western Asset Global Management'.

Despite Curt Livingston's discouragement from past unsuccessful attempts to engage with Duke, I noticed Duke University Pension Plan's interest in U.S. TIPS. I asked Sandy Goodman, a Client Service Executive (CSE), to investigate further. We proceeded with the presentation and won the $200 million assignment.

In March 2000, a team of Credit Suisse First Boston transitioned to Deutsche Bank to establish structured credit programs. This group included Philip Weingord as Managing Director, Mike Lamont as Co-Head, and Richard Kim as Managing Director. Their goal was to create CDOs with large investment firms. Recognizing Ron Mass's expertise at Western Asset Management, Deutsche traders approached him. After several meetings, Ron Mass agreed to manage an asset- backed CDO for Western Asset.

With Ron's commitment, the process of involving Legg Mason and Western Legal and Operations commenced. However, it took over a year to complete the process and secure seed capital.

Deutsche Bank marketing secured a commitment from a large Japanese bank for a significant portion of the required capital, while Legg Mason sales secured a smaller commitment.

For the initial CDO, Western established a warehousing line with Deutsche Bank to manage the asset-backed inventory during compliance, legal, and operational processing. Each asset-backed security purchase had to go to Greg Littman, Deutsche Bank's Global Head of Asset-Backed trading, who had the final say on purchases. Ron and Greg were both seasoned professionals but sometimes disagreed on securities, which prolonged the portfolio setup.

The Confidential Offering Memorandum (COM) was completed pending any last-minute changes. To reassure Legg Mason Credit Committee members about the asset-backed program and those individuals involved, I collaborated with Legg Mason's Dick Himmelfarb, Senior Vice President. We arranged for Deutsche Bank's Philip Weingord and Michael Lamont to attend a Legg Mason Credit meeting at Legg's home office in Baltimore.

Despite addressing concerns during a lengthy meeting, numerous phone calls with Deutsche Bank and Legg Mason the day before closing revisited previously covered details. Late-night discussions, compounded by communication challenges, added tension. Mike Lamont's dead cell led him to hail a cab and search for a functioning payphone in lower Manhattan. As discussions continued late into the night, my team, consisting of Travis Carr and Andrea Mack, managed to secure reservations at Ritz-Carlton Hotel for some much-needed rest. After a few hours, we returned to work to close the deal. Western's first CDO was called 'Arroyo CDO I LTD $400 million', dated August 2001.

In the movie *The Big Short*, Ryan Gosling plays Jared Vennett, a character based on a real person, Greg Lippmann.

After successfully closing the first CDO deal, Western Asset agreed to collaborate with Deutsche Bank on a second CDO in recognition of the effort and time invested in the initial transaction. The second CDO, named 'Pasadena CDO I Ltd' amounted to $500 million and was closed in June 2002. Western Asset secured two additional ABS CDO assignments as a replacement collateral manager (DASH II CDO in November 2002 amounting to $500 million, and Beacon Hill CDO in April 2003, totaling $270 million).

Following the successful initiation of several CDO offerings totaling $1.67 billion, Western Asset Management decided that my involvement in the CDO business was no longer necessary. My CDO responsibilities were transferred to Travis Carr, who worked alongside portfolio manager Ron Mass. Travis Carr had joined the Product Development in December 2000, replacing Scott Mullet.

Additionally, Andrea Mack was transferred from Product Development to the trading desk to manage short-term portfolios. Andrea had replaced Susanne Trepp who worked with Scott and me. Susanne was reassigned as a senior credit analyst on the trading desk. Despite these internal changes, the CDO program remained active and successful, generating new products. These included the Coronado CDO ($500 million) launched in September 2003, followed by the Sierra Madre CDO ($1 billion), and Palisades CDO ($600 million), both introduced in July 2004.

Al McClymonds and I embarked on marketing our relative value fixed income hedge fund program, the San Gabriel Opportunity Fund to potential investors well in advance of its launch, leveraging our connections from our past experiences. One crucial contact was Halbert Lindquist, Senior Manager Director of Hedge Funds at Blackstone Alternative Asset Management (BAAM), whom I had known and worked with previously. During our initial meeting with BAAM, we encountered a diligent analyst who posed numerous questions, and it was only afterward that I recognized her as Carina Baranova, formerly of Schooner Asset Management. Carina had worked with portfolio manager Mark Turner, a renowned global bond manager whom I recommended during my time at EAI Consulting.

Following the meeting, Halbert suggested that I engage Carina to review our Confidential Offering memorandum before finalizing it. This recommendation led to extensive collaboration between Carina, Al, and me to refine the hedge fund document to meet everyone's requirements. Ultimately, BAAM became our third investor and the second significant one, which marked an important milestone for the San Gabriel Opportunity Fund.

On August 6, 2001, Western launched the San Gabriel Opportunity Fund, a relative value fixed income hedge fund with $40 million in seed money from UBS Hong Kong. To support the operational and risk management aspects of the hedge fund, Western Asset's Vern Budinger, Manager of Quantitative Analysis, had been recruited internally.

Vern was a diamond in the rough. He had hedge fund experience in accounting, reporting, and trading and he built our diagnostic systems for reporting from scratch using excel. We compared our system to those of competing hedge funds, and ours was just as good—if not better—than what was commercially available. We received high marks from our customers for our reporting capabilities.

Credit Suisse was selected for the fund's prime brokerage services. John Flint from Credit Suisse played a crucial role in facilitating the launch of the fund. He worked diligently to ensure all necessary documentation was completed and that all operational processes were in place. John provided valuable guidance on operational matters, contributing significantly to the successful start of the San Gabriel Opportunity Fund (SGOF).

Before launching the San Gabriel Opportunity Fund (SGOF), we initiated an internal audit, requesting Western's accounting firm to evaluate our personnel and processes. I first learned about this process during a research trip to London, where institutional, retail, and hedge fund managers operate closely together. The audit recommended that the hedge fund portfolio management team submit a list of securities for review by Western Compliance before executing any transactions. This measure was advised to prevent any possibility of front-running the Western Institutional business.

I presented at a Legg Mason Credit Committee meeting in Baltimore to provide details about the San Gabriel Opportunity Fund (SGOF) and the $40 million in seed capital secured from Dr. Andrew Ho of UBS Hong Kong. The decision to seed a hedge fund with an institutional fixed income, long-only manager like Western Asset Management Company, coupled with securing funding from Hong Kong, prompted significant questions and discussions within the Committee.

During the meeting, I highlighted my year-long pursuit to engage Dr. Andrew Ho from UBS Hong Kong, renowned for seeding successful hedge funds like BlackRock's Obsidian. Dr Ho had previously worked with acclaimed hedge fund manager Mike Vranos of Ellington Capital. He visited Western's office, reviewed our processes, examined our management reports and trades, and scrutinized our portfolio managers' while in New York. Shortly after the launch San Gabriel, Dr. Ho moved his operations to UBS Headquarters in Stamford, CT. Following this, Legg Mason then added me to LM Financial Partners, making me the sole Western person authorized to market and sell SGOF.

Timothy J. O'Grady

117 E. Colorado Blvd.
Pasadena, CA 91105
626-844-9510   Fax: 626-844-9501
togrady@westernasset.com

LM FINANCIAL PARTNERS, INC. — MEMBER NASD/SIPC — A LEGG MASON COMPANY

The San Gabriel Opportunity Fund (SGOF) achieved a net

return of 2.3% in August. Remarkably, the fund continued to perform well in September, earning 1.35%. This made it one of the few hedge funds to add value during the tragic events of the 9/11. Portfolio manager Jai Choi's adept management allowed for strategic adjustments in mortgages immediately following the attacks, which contributed to the fund's success. Overall, SGOF yielded a net return of 8.8% over the four-plus months of 2001.

When marketing the SGOF Fund in 2002, inquiries often arose about its performance during significant market downturns like those in 1974 and 1987. I responded by highlighting that we were not managing funds during those periods. However, I emphasized our resilience and success in the aftermath of 9/11, which resonated well, particularly with prospects who were hesitant to invest regardless.

# 17

# DIRECTOR

My promotion to Director at the end of 2001 came as a surprise, as there had been no prior rumors or indications about such advancements. Joining Western around the same time as Jim Hayes and Steve Fulton, I was pleased with the recognition and the new office. I was mindful that some colleagues who had been at the company longer may have been disappointed not to receive a promotion. Therefore, I chose not to make a big deal about it.

Securing Investcorp Bank B.S.C. Kingdom of Bahrain as an early investor in the San Gabriel Opportunity Fund (SGOF) in 2002 was a significant achievement. I worked with NYC-based Prashant Kolluri, Managing Director, CIO, and his staff to secure the investment. As a multi-billion-dollar investor in hedge funds, Investcorp's participation added credibility and value to SGOF. Moving forward in my investment career, I made a concerted effort to maintain connections with Investcorp.

Fast forward to 2021, my interest in the movie *House of Gucci* led me down an unexpected path of reminiscence. Given the film's Italian setting and its captivating storyline, Investcorp emerged as pivotal in the real-life drama surrounding Gucci's acquisition.

Intrigued by this, I bought the book *The House of Gucci: A Sensational Story of Murder, Madness, Glamour and Greed*. As I progressed through the book, I came across a fascinating story about Investcorp's involvement. A pivotal scene depicted Paul Dimitruk and Rick Swanson of Investcorp meeting Maurizio Gucci at Harry's Bar in London to discuss Investcorp's potential acquisition of the 50% ownership held by Maurizio's uncles and brothers. This meeting ultimately led to Paul Dimitruk being appointed as Gucci's Vice Chairman.

Years later, my own professional journey intersected with this narrative. During my EAI manager trips to London, I met with Paul Dimitruk then serving as Partner, Chairman, and CEO of Pareto Partners. Later, at Partners Capital in Boston, our paths crossed again when I was at ROW Asset Management.

Ronald Layard-Liesching, co-founder and Chief Research Officer of Pareto, and I found ourselves on parallel paths during currency speaker tours across the U.S. and London. Pareto was a recommended currency, currency overlay manager by EAI. Our collaboration reached an unexpected twist during our final presentation together: Currency Overlay Management—Point-Counterpoint was in NYC in November 1998 for AIMR (now CFA Institute).

In a twist of fate, I delivered Ron's portion during the presentation, and he gave mine. Despite the unconventional format the audience responded positively, and the session went off seamlessly. The AIMR conference presentations were subsequently published.

Upon joining Western Asset, I explored the possibility of a joint venture between Pareto's quantitative currency overlay and London global bond management. While historical simulations showed promise, the idea was ultimately rejected by London. Ten years earlier, I had made a similar recommendation to FX Concepts (FXC). PIMCO was working on currency, and I suggested FXC reach out to PIMCO for a joint venture.

Building on the initial successes with CBO's and hedge funds I swiftly transitioned to spearheading a closed-end bond fund project. Western Asset's inaugural closed-end bond fund, the Western Asset Investment Grade Income Fund, debuted on March 22, 1973. With assets under management of $124 million and ticker symbol PAI, it represented a significant milestone for the firm.

Despite the promising start, Western Asset encountered hurdles in launching additional closed-end funds (CEFs) in the following years.

A closed-end fund (CEF) is a type of investment fund that is publicly traded on an exchange, typically the New York Stock exchange, and is primarily sold to retail investors, including individuals and smaller investors. Unlike mutual funds, CEFs have a fixed number of shares and are not redeemable at the option of the shareholder. Additionally, CEFs do not have a minimum investment requirement.

As an institutional bond manager, Western Asset faced challenges venturing into retail public funds arena because Western lacked the typical brand recognition and presence in television marketing or appearances by financial experts often referred to as 'TV Talking Heads'. Despite its success in serving institutional clients, Western Asset fixed income was unknown in retail investment space.

During this period, Merrill Lynch held a dominant position as the leading manager for closed-end funds (CEFs), with many managers turning to them for their expertise and market influence. Western Asset Management maintained a significant business relationship with Merrill, primarily institutional revolving around U.S. Treasury futures on the Chicago Mercantile Exchange (CME). However, despite this robust partnership, Western did not receive preferential treatment in Merrill Lynch's retail investment business.

Merrill's branch managers operated as kings in their own

domains, exercising considerable autonomy and discretion in their decision-making process.

Legg Mason agreed to co-underwrite the closed-end fund effort with Merrill Lynch. Legg Mason's strong reputation in the equity space, particularly due to Bill Miller's remarkable track record of consistently outperforming the S&P 500 Equity Index, lent credibility to the venture. This partnership enhanced Western Asset's position in retail space.

In crafting the name for our closed-end fund (CEF), I was adamant about including 'Premier' to highlight the exceptional quality of our offering, particularly for the public and retail investor market. The chosen title, 'Western Asset Premier Bond Fund' was carefully selected to convey a sense of exclusivity and excellence. Navigating the approval process with the SEC required collaboration with our legal team, led by Brian Chegwidden from Ropes & Gray. Together, we addressed any regulatory concerns and made necessary adjustments to ensure compliance. After these efforts, the SEC granted approval for the name.

During the traditional closed-end fund selling period of two and a half weeks, I traveled along the east coast with Legg Mason's Alexsander Stewart. We visited Legg Mason and Merrill Lynch offices and met with prospective investors who were familiar with CEFs. Additionally, Western Asset portfolio managers delivered presentations at select Merrill Lynch branch offices, coordinated through branch managers.

Raising only $136 million dollars was a major disappointment, especially considering the substantial efforts made by both Legg Mason and Merrill Lynch. Legg Mason managed to raise $65 million through its 1500 financial advisors, while Merrill Lynch achieved a similar result with its 15,000 financial advisors.

The Western Asset Premier Bond Fund, with the ticker symbol 'WEA' opened for trading on March 28, 2002. However, due to its small size there was no traditional ringing of the New York Stock Exchange Bell to mark its opening.

A quote from former Western Asset portfolio manager Ron Mass's CV on LinkedIn shows its success, " I managed Western Asset's top-performing closed-end fund, Western Asset Premier Bond Fund (WEA), from 2002–2012. WEA ranked #2 in its Lipper Closed-End Fund category and produced annualized returns of 9.5% net of fees."

Steve Saruwatari's transition from Accounting to Product Development marked a pivotal moment in our strategic planning for the next closed-end fund (CEF) initiative. Economic conditions, trends in financial markets, and regulatory changes can all influence investor behavior and appetite for particular vehicles like CEFs. My plan was to launch a TIPs CEF because one did not exist and Western had an edge in trading TIPS. But we had to assess the profitability of targeting the CEF market.

In just a few years, Western grew significantly and became a more politically oriented organization as a result. With this transformation came a rigorous approval process for new product ideas, requiring detailed efforts with overwhelming requirements for supporting documentation to secure decisions.

Recognizing this trend, Steve Saruwatari and I collaborated on two papers. The first, a 37-page feasibility study, titled 'Expansion of Western Asset's Closed-End Bond Fund Capabilities', was published on November 12, 2002, and sent to Western's Executive Committee. This study outlined the potential for expanding Western's closed-end bond capabilities and provided a thorough analysis to support the proposal.

In addition, we worked on a second paper focusing on U.S. TIPS competitors. This 10-page detailed report on firms that considered a TIPS product reflected my enthusiasm for TIPS as Western's next-closed-end fund venture.

While not initially included in the closed-end fund study, an aspect we explored was the role of the New York Stock Exchange Specialist firm, Performance Specialist Group. As specialists on the floor of the NYSE, they would facilitate the trading of our CEFs. I met with three New York-based director of communications who arranged for me to visit the NYSE floor to speak to the CEF floor specialists at their post. The main feedback was our CEF should aim to be close to $1 billion in size.

Somewhere along the road to solving our marketing challenges, Steve Saruwatari connected with individuals from Claymore Securities Inc of Wheaton, Illinois. Claymore had a specialization in managing and marketing closed-end funds, which made them an attractive potential partner for Western Asset. Despite Steve's and my desire to develop a new wholesaling operation at Western, management decided to partner with Claymore instead.

Steve Saruwatari, Travis Carr, Western Marketers collaborated with Claymore salesmen on the issuance of two U.S. TIPS closed-end funds:

- Western/Asset Inflation Protected Securities Fund, ticker symbol 'WIA', was launched on September 23, 2003, boosting assets of $220 million, with leverage totaling $361 million.
- Following its success, Western/Asset Inflation Protected Securities Fund 2, identified by the ticker symbol 'WIW', was issued on February 24, 2004. This fund saw assets reach $662 million, with leverage totaling $995 million.

Notably, Western Asset manages the only two TIPS closed-end funds in the market. Barron's has consistently highlighted WIW as an attractive option for investors seeking protection against inflation, underscoring the fund's relevance and appeal within investment landscape.

The transition out of the closed-end fund (CEF) effort by Western management marked a shift in focus toward other projects for me. Meanwhile, Steve Saruwatari got to ring the bell at the opening of the New York Stock Exchange when Fund WIA commenced trading on September 25, 2003. These were the final closed-end funds issued by Western during my tenure.

The NYSE sent me a gift for the second TIPS Closed-End Fund, WIW launched February 2, 2004.

Management also decided that I should transition away from the SGOF hedge fund to work on other new products. June 2002 was the last monthly hedge fund letter that Al McClymonds and I signed. When the July 2002 SGOF letter was issued, it resembled a generic Western Asset fixed income report, and the SGOF marketing materials took on a more generic Western Asset fixed income appearance, which signaled the transition away from SGOF-specific branding.

The shift in responsibilities regarding the hedge fund effort came as a surprise. The closed-end fund and CDO programs were mature and firmly established. With Travis Carr, Steve Saruwatari, and James So—my recent recruit from JP Morgan—overseeing the programs, I felt confident in the team's effective management capabilities. I guess management did also.

The San Gabriel Opportunity Fund witnessed remarkable growth. Two of the initial investors, UBS and Blackstone, eventually committed $150 million each, reaching the maximum investment per firm set by Western Asset. Other notable institutions including Merrill, Citibank, Investcorp, Ontario Teachers, Bank of America, and Mitsubishi were early investors in SGOF with the fund's assets nearing the $1 billion mark.

Building on the success of the San Gabriel Opportunity Fund, Mitsubishi funded the Mitsubishi Opportunity Fund in August 2003, focusing on mortgage investments. Western's Jay Choi was chosen as one of the mortgage managers for this venture, testament to Western's expertise in the field.

As the SGOF franchise began to take shape, Mitsubishi representatives approached Steve Saruwatari and me to discuss an exclusive marketing arrangement in Japan. They had requested an agreement before, and we had passed. We passed again.

In August 2004, Western Asset decided to close the San Gabriel Opportunity Fund. According to a report from the New York Sun dated September 20, 2004, "the San Gabriel Fund had nearly $600 million under management when the decision to close it was made early last month, according to a person familiar with the situation. The decision to shut the San Gabriel Fund was hastened by the departure of its chief portfolio manager, Al McClymonds, who resigned early last month to move back to the East Coast."

Less than a year later, Legg Mason's recognition of our efforts with the San Gabriel Opportunity Fund became evident, as they made a significant acquisition: the purchase of the Permal Group for $1.4 billion. The Permal Group was widely recognized as one of the largest managers of fund of hedge funds globally, overseeing portfolios with assets totaling $20 billion. This acquisition underscored Legg Mason's commitment to expanding its presence and capabilities in the alternative investment space, further validating the strategic direction and success of our endeavors with the San Gabriel Opportunity Fund.

On June 24, 2005, according to the Wall Street Journal, "Citigroup Inc. and Legg Mason Inc. announced an asset-swap deal valued at about $3.7 billion. Under this agreement, Citigroup would relinquish nearly all of its asset-management business in exchange for Legg's brokerage network." This transaction marked a significant shift for Legg Mason, as it expanded its footprint in retail and international businesses, diversifying its offerings and market presence.

During 2005, rumors circulated that Legg Mason was considering expansion into more global locations and retail markets, diverging from its focus on institutional markets. Speculation pointed toward potential acquisitions of Merrill Lynch and Citi Asset Management (CAM).

My familiarity with Citi Asset Management (CAM) managers stemmed from my tenure at EAI Consulting, where CAM owned Smith Barney, a client of ours. Throughout my career, I had interactions with Salomon Brothers during my time at Colonial Bank, Roosevelt & Cross, and EAI Consulting. Given this background, I harbored hopes that Legg Mason might acquire Merrill Lynch, a notion that many Western Asset employees, me included, began exploring. We scrutinized both CAM and Merrill Lynch material to ascertain how either firm could enhance value and speculated on the potential challenges and distractions of a merger.

Given the decision regarding CAM, I anticipated being involved in navigating the mutual funds and closed-end funds of Salomon Brothers, Smith Barney, Legg Mason, and Western Asset.

With my extensive experience with these institutions, I assumed I would naturally take on this responsibility. I began collecting data for the task but halted when someone else was chosen for the assignment.

In 2002 and 2003, amidst the outbreak of the severe acute respiratory syndrome (SARS) epidemic, Blackstone Alternative Asset Management (BAAM) approached Western Asset to explore the possibility of developing a portfolio specifically structured to capitalize on rare, extreme downward market movements—a Tail Protection Fund. I worked with Western's portfolio managers and leveraged my industry connections to investigate potential strategies. Despite our concerted efforts, we were unable to devise a viable product that aligned with our objectives.

In April 2004, BAAM's now Co-CIO Halbert Lindquist initiated the development of a Tail Protection Fund. Hal curated a list of asset managers who he believed could contribute to the success of such fund. Western Asset was approached to manage a credit protection strategy, which entailed synthetic short positions on corporate credits through corporate credit default swaps (CDS). Similar proposals were extended to other managers across various asset classes. However, I hesitated because I recognized the need for assistance in conceptualizing the idea, designing its structure, and navigating the complexities associated with credit default swaps.

The first step I took before initiating any project was consulting Western's legal team, led by Chief Compliance Officer Kevin Ehrlich. Working with Western's legal department was a positive experience; they offered constructive suggestions rather than simply stating limitations. Over coffee at the nearby Bond Market coffee shop, Kevin and I discussed the credit protection strategy. Kevin patiently sketched out the plan on a napkin and redid it a few times while I kept interrupting with questions. With the guidance and expertise of Western's legal and portfolio management teams, I felt confident about moving forward with this unique assignment.

The Western Asset Credit Protection Fund was launched with an initial capital of $36 million from BAAM, leveraging a notional exposure seven times its initial capital amounting to $252 million. To facilitate operations, I enlisted John Flint's assistance in securing Credit Suisse as the funds prime broker. Fund account 4012 was funded on September 1, 2004. We established a CDX benchmark comprising of 85% investment grade and 15% high-yield, based on U.S. credit indices.

BAAM injected an additional $15 million on October 1 and an extra $10 million on November 1. Management fees were calculated based on the notional exposure. A confidential offering memorandum, titled 'Western Asset Credit Protection Fund, Ltd' was issued on October 1, 2004. The original name of the fund was Big Bear Fund but that did not pass compliance, or legal. I proposed the name Western Asset Credit Protection Fund which was ultimately approved.

Copy No. _____

Delivered on _____, _____, to _____

This Confidential Offering Memorandum is not to be photocopied or reproduced in any way, or distributed to anyone, without the express written consent of Western Asset Management Company.

**Confidential Offering Memorandum**

Dated October 1, 2004

Western Asset Credit Protection Fund, Ltd.

Cayman Islands Exempted Company

INVESTMENT MANAGER: WESTERN ASSET MANAGEMENT COMPANY

The performance of the Western Asset Credit Protection Fund declined from 2005 into 2006. The corporate bond portfolio managed by Western did not generate sufficient returns to cover the expenses associated with purchasing and rolling over corporate credit default swaps, also known as credit insurance. Additionally, Western Asset's holdings of General Motors bonds performed poorly, which exacerbated the fund's underperformance. (GM ultimately defaulted in 2009).

BAAM expressed dissatisfaction with the fund's performance, a sentiment that became apparent during a conference call with BAAM investors in which Western portfolio managers and I faced criticism for the fund's shortcomings. Subsequently, I discussed the situation with Halbert Linquist of BAAM, emphasizing the need to end the fund due to its subpar performance.

Halbert, who had not participated in the conference call, requested additional time before deciding. After further deliberation, he put forward a strategy to rescue the Fund. His proposal was to continue rolling the credit default swap contracts while simultaneously adding S&P 500 options trading to corporate bond trading.

Despite the challenges and stress associated with BAAM's involvement in suggesting S&P 500 options trades, I persuaded Western Asset to proceed with the fund. S&P 500 futures and options were in the fund documents. I discussed the situation with John Flint, our prime broker, who acknowledged the use of S&P 500 options in the fund and facilitated the implementation of the proposed strategy.

While some Western bond portfolio managers were eager to terminate the relationship with BAAM, others recognized the importance of maintaining the Tail Protection Fund to fulfill its intended objectives. We decided to continue with the program. This decision reflected a balanced consideration of various perspectives within Western Asset in alignment with our goals and objectives.

When BAAM unexpectedly reached out to request a special trade involving currency options—a 30-day options cross trade, specifically long Australia/short New Zealand currency options—I immediately knew currency options were not covered by credit default guidelines. Acting swiftly, I engaged with Western Compliance, Credit Suisse, the Pasadena Western portfolio manager, and the London Western portfolio manager. Given the urgency of BAAM's request, I worked diligently with all parties to facilitate the trade. The execution was to be handled by the London Western trading desk, where currency trading took place. Despite the unconventional nature of the trade and the need for quick action, I managed to secure approval from all relevant parties to proceed.

Utilizing a significant amount of goodwill within Western Asset, I facilitated the execution of the trade. Coordinating closely with the Western currency desk in London and Goldman Sachs London, the trading partner requested by BAAM, I ensured a seamless collaboration for the trade. The trade commenced on May 11 at around 3:30 a.m. EDT and concluded approximately three hours later at 6:30 a.m. Despite the challenges, the trade was successfully executed as requested, which demonstrated effective teamwork and coordination across multiple parties.

Prior to accepting the BAAM request, I called my son, Ryan O'Grady, to discuss currency options trade. He pointed out that if it involved a $1 billion notional (my estimate from my conversations with BAAM), it would be noticeable on the currency broker screens. Moreover, given that it was a 30-day option, something was likely to happen quickly. A $1 billion notional, costing approximately 1%, would amount to about $10 million dollars. Importantly, it was BAAM money from their portfolio, not Western's funds.

The Bloomberg chart shows the AUD/NZD cross starting May 6, 2006, with direction moving upward until *the trade*. Goldman did a poor job executing it. Notice the drop inside the circled line. There is a bottom on May 17 (not pictured) where enough of the trade was taken off to cover the cost with some gain and on May 25, fourteen days after the 30-day option trade was on, it was removed. Looking at charts of the trade, I'm guessing that in its entirety, the price moved about 4.24% ending at 1.18.

The potential profit from the $1 billion notional trade amounted to approximately $32.4 million gross, factoring in the initial cost of $10 million. However, after accounting for early deductions and option decay, the net profit may have ranged between $20–$25 million. This liquidity was retained in the Western Credit Protection Fund to cover the ongoing expenses associated with the rollover of corporate credit default swaps. Following the trade, I traveled to New York to meet with BAAM and John Flint at Credit Suisse. While BAAM expressed satisfaction with the outcome, I took measures to prevent such occurrences from happening again and to effectively maintain operational integrity moving forward.

Many years later, around 2015, I found myself at ROW Asset Management presenting to John Smith, Senior Portfolio Manager at USB Alternative and Quantitative Investments. During a casual conversation with John, I asked him to inquire with his boss, Bruce Amlicke (CIO at UBS Hedge Fund Solutions), if he remembered a particular time as Co-CIO at BAAM. It involved a cross-currency

AUD/NZD trade, which proved to be highly profitable. To my surprise, Bruce remembered the event, recalling working with O'Grady from a California firm.

I had always held a strong belief in the Tail Protection concept which the BAAM-Western Asset Credit Protection Fund exemplified. It was not only highly profitable for BAAM but also served as source of management fees for Western. However, as this fund operated within the realm of hedge funds, there was never any marketing effort or discussion around it. Moreover, since Western's domestic fixed income performance suffered during the market decline, it was best not to discuss the success of the Tail Fund. I was not privy to the exact amount of revenue generated by the Tail Protection Fund as I had moved on from the fund responsibilities after management tasked me with other responsibilities.

In March of 2006, Western's CEO Jim Hirschmann was appointed President of Legg Mason, Baltimore. Following this, Dan Fleet assumed the role of President of Western, in addition to his responsibilities for overseeing the integration of Legg Mason/Western Asset/CAM. Having joined Western Asset in 1999, a few months after Dan, I was familiar with him and felt optimistic about his leadership in the integration process. I would join Dan shortly in his Corporate Strategy/Product Development Group eager to contribute to the organization's continued success under his leadership.

Legg Mason had a series of funds managed by its various investment firms, including Western Asset, Clearbridge Investments, Brandywine Global Investments, and Royce & Associates. Each firm brought its unique expertise to the table. I assumed that the overlap of funds from these managers had been addressed during the fund review process following the acquisition to ensure each fund had a distinct purpose and to remove redundancy within the family.

Dan asked me to go to Western's (formerly CAM's) New York

office to review and suggest any new offering that we should be considering. However, given the recent fund reduction and amalgamation, the NYC office was not keen on discussing anything new. Despite this reluctance, I remained determined to find innovative solutions that would complement our existing lineup without overlapping with the streamlined offerings.

In the beginning of 2006, Western Asset Management held the distinction of being the largest fixed income firm globally, surpassing competitors like PIMCO and BlackRock. However, this title was short-lived as PIMCO suddenly got bigger, and BlackRock's acquired of Merrill Lynch.

I called some of my street contacts to ask what was selling in fixed income retail space. The reply: "Large bond firms we were trying to create fixed income mutual funds for Separately Managed Accounts (SMAs)." A Separately Managed Account (SMA) typically comprises individual issues rather than mutual funds or a combination thereof. Most SMAs are small in size, which makes diversifying with a combination of individual issues costly, and far too expensive to have a combination of individual issues and mutual funds. Management fees for SMAs are typically around 1%; retail mutual funds have heavy fees; many have front end loaded fees.

I did what I did back in 1968 at Winchester Western Firearms Company. I called competitors to find out about their new product lines. In this case, I never used the Tim O'Grady; instead, I used the names of friends or people I particularly did not like.

Our competitors were working on institutional managed fixed-income mutual funds tailored specifically for Separately Managed Accounts (SMA's) and exclusively for SMAs. These fixed- income mutual funds would be complemented by individual equity securities, offering a broader range of opportunities than just individual issues, thereby enhancing the appeal of SMAs. Additionally, these firms were collaborating with the SEC on the pricing of these

SMA-targeted mutual funds, ensuring compliance and transparency in the pricing process.

PIMCO was a pioneer in this space with the creation of PIMCO Fixed Income Shares (FISH), while BlackRock used the name Custom Managed Account Portfolios (CMAP). I sought the opinions of the CAM-Smith Barney and Legg retail brokers on the concept of an SMA combining individual issues with bond mutual funds at a reasonable management fee. However, to my surprise, there was little enthusiasm for the idea. It appeared that the PIMCO Fixed Income Shares, FISH, had not made a significant impact in the industry.

My son James, who has built a business through hard work, has a saying, "It is impossible to assemble a puzzle without looking at the box. You need to see what you are aiming for." Despite some lack of enthusiasm, I believed that a Separately Managed Account (SMA) with a series of Western funds was a terrific idea. By adding slices of mortgages, corporates, high yield, and high-yield municipals through various funds, we could offer a diverse menu for retail investors. This would allow them to create their own asset allocation with professionally managed fixed income.

However, I was concerned that the term 'high yield' might not attract investors, so I rebranded high-yield corporates as 'Extended Credit' and high-yield municipals as 'Municipal Extended Credit'. CAM NYC already had a well-established reputation in municipal bonds, so I simply extended their menu.

Normally, I would have a name for the product myself but this time I got help from Steve Saruwatari. We have been referring to the product as SMA shares in our discussions. Steve suggested 'SMASh Series Funds' or simply 'SMASh'! Nobody had the name, so our new retail entry became SMASh. I checked with CAM-NYC about the name—they hated it. Perfect!

Now we had to deal with the SEC regarding the total fees charged when combining individual issues with a mutual fund or a series of mutual funds. I consulted Ropes & Gray to determine the SMA fee that the SEC would permit in such a scenario. This marked the beginning of a year-long collaboration with Ropes & Gray's Boston legal team, during which we drafted a fee substantiation memo outlining Western Asset's implied fee calculation for the Legg Mason Partners SMASh Series Funds. The preparation of this memo incurred a cost of approximately $500,000.

Although CAM NYC was not fond of SMASh, the favored 'Kicker Funds' the newly created Western Asset Funds tailored specifically for SMAs was a hit. These new funds were not available for separate purchase.

We introduced four new mutual funds in our prospectus (below):

**SMASh M** Fund-Mortgages

**SMASh C** Fund-Investment Grade Corporates

**SMASh EC** Fund-Extended Credit Corporates (high yield)

**SMASh MEC** Fund-Municipal Extended Credit (municipal high yield).

To support our fee recommendation, we had to forecast the expected AUM for each of the Kicker Funds over a five-year period. Additionally, we outlined the fee split between Legg Mason and Western Asset. The prospectus was dated April 16, 2007, then amended as of June 7, 2007. I selected June 7 because it coincided with my birthday—a happy sixty-two to me. This milestone added a touch of personal celebration to the professional achievements involved in the project.

Years later I got a call from a friend at Western. He said,

"Remember the SMASh Fund M, ticker symbol LMSMX. It surpassed $3 billion in AUM, making it the largest SMA fund."

The underperformance of Western Asset Management's investment programs during the turbulent years of 2007–2009 was a significant challenge for the organization. In response to the negative trends and market conditions, the company had to make tough decisions, including layoffs.

On Monday afternoon March 23, 2009, after lunch, I was called into President Dan Fleet's office. To my surprise, I was informed that the Corporate Strategy & Product Development Group was being shut down, resulting in the termination of my employment. Dan himself would retire within a few months.

The news came as a shock, especially considering the positive feedback I received for my work, particularly the launch of the SMASh Funds in 2007. Additionally, in 2008, I had been involved in significant projects, including a quantitative currency program with the Tokyo Office. My former partner, Steve Saruwatari, had been transferred to Tokyo to work on new products with Kazuto Doi, Head of investment Management in Tokyo.

Kazuko Doi joined Western Asset Management as part of the Citigroup Asset Management (CAM) acquisition. Before his tenure at CAM Tokyo, he served as an Investment Research Manager at PanAgora Asset Management. During my time with EAI, PanAgora's Alan Brown, based in London, was on the EAI's recommended list of global bonds managers. This connection gave me a solid understanding of the quantitative processes behind Kazuto's currency programs.

I was able to use my office and phone until the end of the month to unwind all the connections I had with clients and brokers. But that Monday afternoon, I just wanted to go home. Lorraine had driven me to work that day because she had a movie shot scheduled in Pasadena. The set was a large parking lot on the corner of East Colorado Blvd and Orange Grove Street. If you ever watched the Rose Bowl Parade on New Year's Day, you might recognize that first camera shot of the parade is on Orange Grove Street, where the parade makes a right turn onto East Colorado Blvd., also known as The Historic Route 66.

Grant Schick, a colleague from the Corporate Strategy & Product Group gave me a ride to the set. Sensing my mood, Lorraine decided that we were both done for the day.

# 18

# HOLLYWOOD

Lorraine and I were eager to experience being in the audience and being seen on television long before our move to California. The *Tonight Show* starring Johnny Carson was originally filmed live at 30 Rockefeller Plaza in New York City from 1962–1972 relocating to Burbank, CA. The live taping occurred from 6:00–7:30 p.m. EDST, with the show airing nationally 11:30 p.m.–1:00 a.m. EDST. Securing tickets for the show was no easy feat, as it took months of effort and required arriving at NBC Studios well in advance of the taping. TV studios always issued more tickets than seats to ensure a full audience. Once inside the studio, the challenge was to guess where the camera would pan during commercial breaks. Our first visit saw us making a rookie mistake, choosing seats that ended up empty because the camera panned over your heads. However, on our second attempt, we adopted a more strategic approach and managed to secure better seats. We were thrilled to see ourselves on camera as it panned across the audience during commercial breaks.

The energy of the show, with Johnny Carson, Ed McMahon, and the NBC Orchestra led by Doc Severinsen, was electric. After taping, we rushed home to call friends and family, asking them to tune in to see us during the commercial breaks. It was a few seconds of fun done in an era before the availability of TV recording technology. If you blinked, you missed us.

Shortly after moving to California, Lorraine joined Entertainment Partners 'Central Casting' as a non-union background extra. While there are several casting agencies near Los Angeles, Central Casting is renowned as the largest and best-known casting agency in the industry.

Lorraine had an exciting opportunity to appear on the TV show ER through Central Casting. Although her character would not be fully exposed, Lorraine was required to be semi-naked with a prosthesis on. To maintain modesty, she was provided with a tube top, girdle piece, and a robe to wear under the hospital gown. On set, she lay on an emergency room table with a cut-out for her torso, allowing the prosthetic chest to be positioned above. Carefully placed EKG leads and additional props, like a fake IV tube and a ventilator tube taped into her mouth, completed the scene.

In the scene, the doctor, played by Goran Visnjic, repeatedly attempted to revive Lorraine's character with electric paddles, while an EMT performed chest compressions. After several minutes of intense effort, her character was declared dead at '9:37'. Despite the scene lasting only a few minutes on screen, it took one and a half hours to shoot from all angles. Lorraine had to act convincingly, arching up each time she was 'zapped'. she received extra compensation for her efforts.

Three years later, I decided to join Lorraine in her pursuit of acting gigs and registered at Central Casting. We frequently called the Central Casting work line, each hoping to be added to upcoming projects. Lorraine struck gold with the opportunity to work on the new movie *The Holiday*, boasting a star-studded cast including Cameron Diaz, Jude Law, Kate Winslet, Jack Black, and Eli Wallach. We attended a fitting on January 5 to ensure we had the right wardrobe for our roles, and shooting took place on January 13 and 16. I even took two vacation days from my job at Western Asset to participate. Directed, written, and co-produced by Nancy Meyers, who was known for her meticulous attention to detail, often required shooting scenes multiple times. We both made brief appearances on the big screen in a scene shot in a local school auditorium where Eli Wallach walks up onto the stage and to receive a long overdue writing award.

Before filming, staff took Kodak pictures of the audience seating, anticipating breaks during filming. Consistency was crucial across shots. During the first break, panic ensued over an open seat. It turned out the occupant had fallen ill, calming worries.

Working on a movie set, you quickly learn that the assistant director or 1st AD is the linchpin bridging the director and crew. Second assistant directors (2nd AD) work directly under the 1st AD, akin to army sergeants enforcing orders and directives. However, changes on the set are often fluid, and many times the 2nd ADs lack a clear understanding of the director's vision. Even the director may be uncertain at times, despite having the script pages for the day's shoot. It requires thick skin to handle the young, entitled individuals with big egos who may yell at you to do something, only to change their minds later. The most challenging aspect is working in a group that has never collaborated before, sometimes spending hours waiting for a scene to be set up. The ADs are always under pressure to prepare the set promptly because time is money in the film industry.

Getting on camera on a movie set is competitive. Rule #1: find where the cameras will be and position yourself strategically near or behind the stars. Shots are taken at different angles, which makes it a guessing game. With everyone vying 'face time', there's pushing and shoving and cutting in line. On set, nobody is your friend because opportunities to be on camera are scarce, as the focus will always be on the actors.

For the Eli Wallach writing award scene, Lorraine and I strategically positioned ourselves in the audience directly behind and two seats over to the right of stars Jack Black and Kate Winslet; Kate sat on the aisle. We guessed their seats before they were positioned and situated ourselves as close behind as possible. Fortunately, our camera shot was taken from the back of the stage capturing the audience. In the scene where Eli Wallach gives an acceptance speech, the backstage camera focuses on Jack Black and Kate Winslet in the audience, with us visible behind them. *The Holiday* has become a Christmas Classic!

Whenever I am out to dinner with my grandkids during the holidays, I put a napkin over my head, held on by my eyeglasses and I become Mr. Napkin Head, just as Jude Law did in *The Holiday*.

More than a year later, while driving home from work in Pasadena, I received a call on my cell phone from J.J., an agent from Central Casting. He requested me to come in and bring my portfolio for a part in *The Closer*, a TV show starring Kyra Sedgwick, J.K Simmons, G.W Bailey, Tony Denison, and others. The role was for a dead Irish cop named Ray Hodge. Interestingly, a staff member on *The Closer* had picked my picture out of Central Casting photos and wanted me for the part.

Driving on the congested 110 highway through Los Angeles during rush hour, I was unable to take any notes. Moreover, I did not have a portfolio of pictures, so I pushed back slightly because Central Casting typically does not make calls; individuals contact them frequently. However, J.J. informed me that there would be three SAG Vouchers for me. SAG stands for Screen Actors Guild, and nonunion background actors can join the union if they earn three vouchers. *The Closer* was going to give me three SAG vouchers to portray dead Ray Hodge enabling me to become a union background extra and earn significantly higher pay.

Agreeing to call J.J. back was a prudent move on my part, especially since I was driving without access to a calendar. It served as the best stall tactic under the circumstances. Once I reached home, Lorraine was surprised that I was called but encouraged me to seize the chance, especially considering the offer of three SAG Vouchers. I returned J.J.'s call from home to obtain directions to Raleigh Studios in Hollywood for March 15, 2007. J.J. even mentioned the possibility of my name appearing in the credits, which added to the excitement. I informed Western Asset that I was going to work from home that day.

Upon arriving at the studio, I parked and made my way to meet the casting person *The Closer* who needed to ensure that I fit the role of a dead Irish cop. After a bit of waiting, during which several others came and went, I began to realize that there might be multiple candidates for the role. Finally, the casting person entered, took a look at me, and promptly approved, saying, "Yes, great, you'll do." I was then introduced to a group of guys who arrived after me and would serve as my fellow pallbearers. Following that, I was directed to another staff member who escorted me to hair and makeup for some photographs to be taken.

I was dressed in a police uniform for the photographs. They mentioned that one of the pictures taken of me in a uniform would be enlarged and used at my character's funeral. Additionally, I had to promise to promptly provide a photo of myself in civilian attire, which would also be enlarged and used at the funeral scene.

The shooting for *The Closer*, 'Morgue/Autopsy Scene'- 'Saving Face, Episode #303, Season Three' took place on March 20 at Raleigh Studios.

I arrived promptly at 8:30 a.m. and was directed straight to the makeup trailer, which was fit for a movie star, on the set. My 'co-star', the deceased woman, and I were joined by Steve, a makeup artist whose task was to transform us for our 'morgue shot'. Steve meticulously created the 'Y' incision on my chest, mimicking an autopsy and gave my face a pallid, grayish look. It took a few hours to achieve the desired autopsy look.

One of the perks of being in a star trailer was the special treatment. My co-star mentioned she was hungry, and shortly after, someone brought us lunch.

After lunch, we were called to the set, so I threw on a bathrobe and made my way to begin filming. Upon entering the set, I was instructed to remove the robe and climb onto the morgue/autopsy room gurney. That's when someone exclaimed, "Do they know you are here!" The entire set froze, and the director or the first assistant director (1st AD) approached me, along with cameraman John Waldo, who had made the exclamation. John explained that we knew each other from working out at Bodies In Motion Kick Boxing in Pasadena each morning. We quickly diffused the situation, and surprisingly, I gained some extra credibility for knowing John Waldo.

The camera then captured several scenes with me, and there was a break to reposition the cameras. During the break, I relaxed on the gurney and enjoyed a soda. John gave me a copy of *The Closer* sides (next to my picture) which detailed the scenes to be shot that day. The sides were small enough to fit into my back pocket, alongside my cell phone.

Standing right next to me was Kyra Sedgwick, the leading star of the show, who engaged in conversation with someone about her husband, movie star Kevin Bacon. Kyra noticed me listening and asked my opinion. I agreed with her, and we exchanged a few brief words before filming resumed.

Later I was informed that I should avoid engaging with the 'principals', which I would hear repeatedly throughout my short stint in the movie industry.

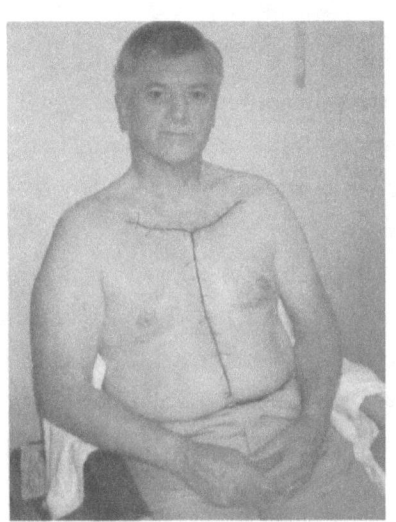
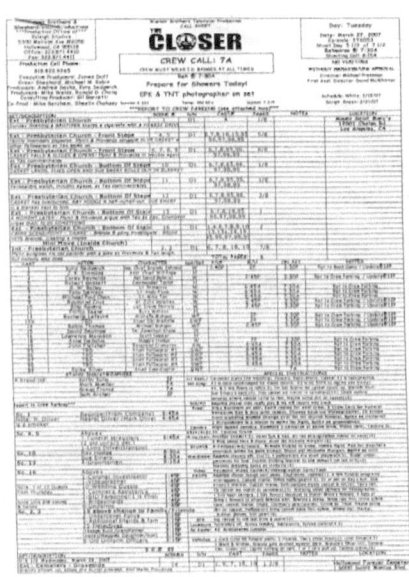

*The Closer* 'Funeral Scene' was shot a week later, on March 27 at Mount St. Mary's College in Brentwood, California. It was an early start, with an all-day shoot planned to ensure completion before sunset. Lorraine had been reading through *The Closer* production script that I received after the 'Morgue Scene' so that I would be prepared for what to expect at the 'Funeral Scene' a week later. When she reached page three, which described the scene involving a casket, Lorraine felt compelled to be present for this filming.

Policemen Flynn and Provenza reach the overturned casket and are stunned to see.......

....seventy-year-old Ray Hodge lying half in and half out of the coffin and, not too far away, a buxom blond WOMAN almost completely unwrapped from the yellow blanket. She is beautiful, she is naked, and she is dead.

The Closer EP. 303-Production Draft-3/16/07

I knew I would be portraying a deceased character in a casket alongside the young actress because the crew discussed testing the casket drop early in the morning to ensure the scene's authenticity. They dropped three empty caskets down the church stairs to achieve realism, which underscored the importance of this moment in the film. My costume that day was a somber funeral suit, and with additional makeup aimed to enhance the appearance of being deceased. It was a unique challenge, but one that added depth to the portrayal of the character.

Meanwhile, Lorraine decided to participate as a mourner in the church funeral scene, dressed appropriately in a dark dress. During one of the breaks, I arranged for one of *The Closer* staff to capture a poignant moment—a picture of the deceased woman, 'Dead Ray' (my character), and the mourner (Lorraine).

The church funeral scene was incredibly lifelike, with a closed casket surrounded by abundant flowers and two large pictures of me, portraying me both as a policeman and a civilian. The atmosphere was eerily realistic, complete with a printed program and an actual service.

The preparation for me 'falling out of the casket' scene involved rehearsals with the team. Lorraine accompanied me to ensure I did not feel claustrophobic being in a casket with a 'nude woman'. Despite a tight fit, I declined an offer of a stand-in. Once the casket top was closed, the darkness inside was palpable. We practiced the maneuver of rolling out of the casket several times until I suggested a slight modification: placing my hand behind the woman as we entered the casket so I could roll her out when the time came. This adjustment worked seamlessly.

In live action, the casket top opened, revealing the woman emerging while I remained halfway in and halfway out. Initially, I was supposed to roll out completely, but practical considerations led us to settle on the half-in, half-out arrangement, which ultimately proved effective. It was an unexpected opportunity for me to exercise some directing influence—a memorable experience indeed.

About a month later, I reached out to *The Closer* show to inquire about obtaining the two large funeral pictures. I was promised the two pictures after the "show was done and, in the can". Eventually, we received the promised pictures, and we proudly hung them in my office at our oceanfront home. Interestingly, workers who visit our house assume I am a cop 'on the take' living in luxurious oceanfront residence, all based on the impression conveyed by those pictures.

Eventually, Lorraine and I purchased two Hollywood Walk of Fame plaques to hang in our home; a plaque for the movies and a plaque for TV. They hang on our wall, not in cement on the Hollywood Walk of Fame (See Appendix for our Hollywood Walk of Fame plaques).

I did not get my three SAG vouchers! I got two instead. On April 2, 2007, I wrote a letter to Membership Eligibility, Screen

Actors Guild (SAG) 5757 Wilshire Blvd. LA 90036. I checked the SAG website, and I was not SAG eligible. I called their office and was told they had me for only two dates March 20 and 27; two does not qualify. I was told to write to them and send all my paperwork, which I did. I got a letter back. I was not given credit for the March 15th day because I did not work, no filming. I had pictures taken. I did not get my name in the credits!

SAG was sorry but only two SAG vouchers. Then the responder suggested that I should think about joining the SAG union because as a union member I am required to work many days a year. And those days are hard to get because about two thirds of those selected for a job are non- union. If this was not a full-time occupation (he knew it was not) then you are better off being non-union to have a better chance for work. The Closer was my second Hollywood job; it was Lorraine's 113th. The next time we worked together was for the movie *The Changeling*, my 3rd and Lorraine's 128th Hollywood performance.

*The Changeling*, shot in November 2007, with Clint Eastwood co-directing and Angelina Jolie starring, provided an exhilarating experience. Our filming day was November 12, starting bright and early at 6:30 a.m. in downtown Los Angeles. Clint's preference for an early start helped avoid traffic and ensured a focused shoot.

Given the period setting of the film, wardrobe requirements were specific, with attire reminiscent of the 1920s. Women adorned coats, dresses, hats, and black shoes, while men sported farmer's outfits. I even had to get a haircut, despite being provided with a hat to wear. Lorraine and I played the role of protesters. Clint's efficiency on set translated into a fast-paced day, with minimal shots needed for each sequence. The attention to detail, from wardrobe to hairstyles, contributed to the authenticity of the production.

On the set of *The Changeling*, adherence to protocol was paramount. Photography and discussions about the film were strictly prohibited, and interacting with actors was discouraged. Our scene involved a protest at Los Angeles City Hall, reminiscent of iconic moments from shows like *Dragnet*. Interestingly, we were instructed not to use profanity during the protest; instead, we could only vocalize our disapproval by shouting "Boo" at the police. On a signal, we ran up the stairs to City Hall, yelling. We were told not to look back at the camera, but to look straight ahead. Clint Eastwood and the camera crew were right behind us. That was take #1.

During a break between takes, I had a surprising encounter with Angelina Jolie. Feeling a hand on my shoulder, I turned to find myself face to face with her. She smiled and politely excused herself. I moved to let her through to go back down the steps. Then were told to go back down the steps and get ready to take #2. I did not wash that shoulder for a few weeks!

Following our scene at City Hall, Lorraine had another opportunity to participate in a *Changeling* shot four days later at Universal Studios as a pedestrian. This time, Clint had his cockatoo with him, which added a unique element to the experience.

The writer's strike at the end of 2007, first quarter 2008 stopped Hollywood film production.

In May 2008, I received an unexpected opportunity to appear in the popular TV comedy show *Entourage*, which was in its 5th season. Travis from Central Casting reached out to me, informing me of a two-day shoot for the second episode of 2008, titled *Unlike a Virgin*, featuring Tony Bennett. It was a thrilling prospect, especially considering the show's widespread acclaim.

For the shoot, I was assigned to wear a grey suit on the first day (May 5) and a tuxedo on the second day (May 6). The filming took place at the historic Orpheum Theater at 842 S. Broadway in downtown Los Angeles. I was promised a SAG voucher.

On the first day of shooting, the set was bustling with energy as it was arranged to resemble a wrap party for Tony Bennett after completing filming a music video. Our instructions were to mingle and move around as if we were guests at the party. Upon entering, I spotted Tony Bennett seated at a table surrounded by a group of young ladies. Seizing the opportunity to potentially appear on camera, I walked right up to him. To my delight, Tony greeted me warmly, reached out, and shook my hand. We exchanged a few words about the video shoot. However, I soon sensed the need to move along as the set was crowded, and my time for interaction was limited.

Throughout the shoot, I strategically positioned myself, anticipating where the cameras might be and engaging in conversations with others as I made my way around the set. During a break, I even managed to snag a seat in the chairs labeled with the names of the show's starts, Vincent Chase, and Turtle, although I could not convince anyone to take my picture.

The second day brought a different scene, as I donned my tuxedo for a stage dancing sequence with another background extra on stage while Tony Bennett performed. It was an exhilarating experience, and I could not wait to share it with my colleagues at Western Asset. The episode aired on September 4, 2008, and my friends at work eagerly tuned in to watch *Entourage*.

## 19

## THANK YOU AND GOODBYE!

'QUI TRANSTULIT SUSTINET'—the State of Connecticut motto translates to 'he who is transplanted still sustains' or 'thrive where you are transplanted'.

I sent an email to my friends at Western and Wall Street, thanking them for their help and support. Inspired by my wife's theme of 'thrive where you are transplanted', I began seeking a new career at sixty-four years, ready for the next chapter.

On our drive home from Pasadena that Monday, March 23, Lorraine took the initiative to call Central Casting's woman's non-union work line. With me at the wheel, she seized the opportunity to explore potential roles. It turned out that there were openings for a new movie, *Iron Man 2*, a Marvel Comics film starring Robert Downey Jr. and Gwyneth Paltrow, directed by Jon Favreau.

Lorraine spoke with Claire, a familiar contact from past Central Casting bookings, and successfully secured a spot. Encouraged by her success, she handed me the phone and urged me to call the men's line immediately. I made the call and was also selected for a role. The next day, March 24, we attended a fitting in Hawthorne, CA. We were excited to be part of such a high-profile production and eagerly prepared for our roles in *Iron Man 2*.

We were scheduled for the first two days of filming, April 6 & 7 and were told to expect long days. The set, designed to represent a U.S. Senate Armed Services Committee meeting, was located at the Masonic Temple on South Euclid Avenue in downtown Pasadena. To better understand the characters and context of the sequel, we watched the first *Iron Man* film beforehand.

During my fitting, my gray business suit and white shirt were approved, but my blue tie did not meet the wardrobe standards. They provided me with a red tie instead. This was surprising for both Lorraine and me, as red is usually avoided in background scenes to prevent distractions. Typically, no red clothing or cars are used.

On April 6 we arrived, checked in, and signed our vouchers before heading to hair and make-up. Once prepared, a 1st AD or a 2nd AD approved our 'senate look' before we began scouting out the senate auditorium, trying to anticipate where the principals would sit. I specifically looked for the video village, situated at the back of the auditorium, where the 1st AD, 2nd AD, and other essential crew members are stationed, along with the monitors.

I also surveyed the stage platform where the senators would be seated noting their position to the right of the judge's bench. Additionally, I spotted the camera setup high behind the stage. The counsel tables were set up in the 'well' between the stage platform and the guest seating. The defendant's table positioned on the left aisle facing the stage, and the plaintiff's table on the right. My familiarity with courtroom setups, thanks to watching shows like *Perry Mason* in high school, proved useful in understanding the layout.

To ensure visibility on camera, Lorraine and I strategically positioned ourselves on the left aisle, not too far back from the front. We aimed to avoid obstruction by the lawyers but remain within the camera's view. A blocked seat on the aisle in front of me suggested that a principal might occupy it. As expected, Gwyneth Paltrow (*Pepper Potts*) took that seat. To avoid having two people with similar hair colors sitting together, Lorraine with her reddish-blond hair, was relocated behind me to the left.

Before filming began on the first day, Jon Favreau, who served as both the director and a character in the film (*Happy Hogan*), took time to introduce himself and provide insights into the scene and characters. Senator Stern's desire for the Iron Man suit for the American people created a central conflict, as Tony Stark and the suit embodied Iron Man.

Our scene unfolds with a shot of the U.S. Capital Building Dome about twenty minutes into *Iron Man 2*. The camera then pans to reveal the senators, the audience, and me sporting my distinctive red tie. Senator Stern (Gary Shandling) subpoenas Tony Stark for questioning by the Armed Services Committee, which set the stage for subsequent events.

In most shots, I was prominently visible, as the camera angles changed. There was a brief pause in the shooting when Gary Shandling needed a moment to collect himself and recall his lines, a common occurrence on sets. Robert Downey Jr. initiated the break, as can be seen in the picture with Jon Favreau discussing the shot. I am shown here under Jon's left arm.

Robert Downey Jr. lightened the mood by getting up on the lawyer's desk and dancing around in the high heel boots, aiming to ease the tension. After Gary regained his composure, he delivered an exceptional performance.

Near the end of the movie shoot, there is a scene where Robert Downey Jr's character walks out on the Senate. In the scene, he stops right next to me in the aisle and we shake hands; then we hug in the next shot; after that, we exchange high fives. We kept retaking the scene until Jon Favreau, the director, was satisfied with the performance. This process continued for a while until Jon finally called 'cut'.

I am featured in the first trailer for the film, and my picture even made it into *Mad* magazine, as seen in the picture next to Robert Downey's left shoulder. Our nephew in Australia spotted it and sent it around.

*Mad Magazine*

During a break, I had the opportunity to chat with Gwyneth Paltrow who discussed her schedule with Tony. Robert Downey Jr. shared his journey of staying clean from drugs, acknowledging the difficulty of the process. As day two concluded, I approached the video village about the footage from the two-day shoot and learned that about ten minutes of the film would feature our scenes. I would be prominently visible throughout. Though I did not keep track of the minutes, the experience itself was unforgettable.

In eight movies following *Iron Man 2*, I did not land any screen time. However, in 2011, I aimed for a screenshot during an NCIS shoot at the Los Angeles Coliseum stadium, USC's home football stadium. This massive undertaking involved 600 people—a 'cattle call'. I never participated in filming where hundreds of people are required. But my admiration for Mark Harmon and NCIS prompted Lorraine to sign up. During the shoot, I strategically positioned ourselves for a shot with Mark Harmon (Gibb) and Cote de Pablo (Ziva David). Just before the camera set up, Ziva suggested relocating it down the aisle. During a break, Mark

Harmon saw us while walking around and came over, greeted Lorraine and me, and inquired about our experience.

Another scene had about fifty of us walking near one of the stadium entrances as Gibb, Ziva, and Tim McGee entered. Our task was to walk around them. I walked straight toward Gibb, then turned right at the last minute just to get my back on the camera. I did not glance up to see if he recognized me from our earlier interaction.

Missing out on an opportunity to work on *Mad Men* starring Jon Hamm was a disappointment for me. Set in 1960s New York City advertising firms, the show was something I really wanted to be part of. Unfortunately, I was in Chicago working at a conference for FX Concepts and could not make the date. Central Casting called and wanted me for a part in the film. They described the role and urged me to come in quickly, but I had to pass due to my prior commitment. When they called again the next day, I explained my situation once more, but it seemed they were displeased with my response. I never received another call from them. Balancing work commitments and acting opportunities eventually led me to step away from the industry in 2014, particularly when I began working for my son in Newport Beach, California.

## 20

# FX CONCEPTS

Jim Conklin, Ph.D., joined FX Concepts (FXC) in the summer of 2008, recruited by Jeffrey Weiser and Ryan O'Grady. Ryan played a pivotal role in creating and programing FX Concepts Global Currency Program (GCP). Jeff managed GCP, which was instrumental in growing GCP's funds from an initial $10 million portfolio to over $8 billion in AUM. Jim was considered a potential successor to Ryan as Head of Investment Research. Jeff Weiser left FX Concepts in February 2009, followed by Ryan's departure in June 2009.

At Fortress Management in NYC, Jim collaborated with Martin Hlusek, an external research consultant from Prague, on developing an alternative fixed income program using forward starting interest rate swaps. Based in Prague, Czech Republic, Martin served as a consultant to Fortress, focusing on swap programs and trading ideas. With a Ph.D. and extensive programming experience, Martin played a key role in the implementation.

While networking in NYC, Ryan suggested I meet with John Taylor, CEO and founder of FX Concepts, about a potential marketing role within a new fixed income group. FXC was planning to develop a fixed income product using interest rate swaps. I managed to secure a meeting with John Taylor, where he briefed me on the startup process and funding. However, President Phil Simotas was unavailable, and John needed Phil to confirm my fit for the marketing, and client service role. After several conference calls, it was agreed that I would start on October 1, 2009, on a two-year contract to develop the forward interest rate swaps program's marketing strategy.

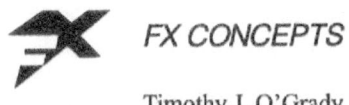

**FX CONCEPTS**

Timothy J. O'Grady
MANAGING DIRECTOR FIXED INCOME

14 PENN PLAZA, NEW YORK, NY 10122
TEL: (212) 554-6846   FAX: (212) 554-6903
E-MAIL ADDRESS: togrady@fx-concepts.com
WEB ADDRESS: www.fx-concepts.com

On October 1, 2009, my inaugural day at FX Concepts, I found myself thrust into the heart of the action. Before diving into the day's agenda, I met with Jim Conklin just before we headed into a meeting with one of FX Concepts' clients, the Government of Singapore Investment Corporation (GIC). The GIC, a sovereign wealth fund with assets totaling billions of dollars, had representatives from both New York City and Singapore visiting their East Coast investment managers. Unfortunately, FX Concepts' flagship fund, Global Currency Program (GCP), would end in 2009 with a disappointing performance of -17.9%.

Amid discussions about challenging currency performance during the meeting, Jim Conklin, Phil Simotas, and I seized the moment to unveil our Global Rates Alpha (GRA) concept. Each of us presented our perspectives on the program, differing on the number of global interest rates included. To streamline the presentation, I deferred to Jim and Phil to discuss the GRA program details. GRA was an innovative fixed income strategy using forward-starting interest rate swaps to strategically position various points along the yield curve. While the GIC representatives listened to our presentation, their primary focus remained on the currency performance of GCP.

After our meeting with GIC, Jim and I grabbed a drink. It was clear that Jim had a lot on his plate, from fine tuning currency models to addressing performance issues to overseeing the complex programming of forward-starting interest rate swaps. He seemed to be juggling multiple responsibilities and was not quite ready to onboard a marketing professional yet.

Jim's familiarity with my background was limited to my connection as Ryan's father. He had his own ideas about assembling his team for derivative marketing, expressing doubts about my understanding of advanced concepts like Principal Component Analysis (PCA). He was correct—PCA was unfamiliar territory to me, and even now, it remains a puzzle. Despite my efforts, I struggled to find anyone to explain PCA to me, except for my son Ryan.

This was another opportunity where my role was defined, but the rest of the cast had not been onboarded or established. Additionally, months after I started, there was no program introduction of GRA at the monthly FXC client calls.

I prepared extensively before joining FX Concepts, much like I had for my roles at the bank, Roosevelt & Cross, EAI Research, and Western Asset. Launching a new idea or new product is a grind, but I did not worry about the most important part: seed money. I trusted that world's largest independent currency firm would secure a client to fund the new concept.

I had the program name in my head on the way home from the interview: Global Rates Alpha, GRA. Inspired by my success at EAI promoting international bonds and currency, the name started with 'G' for Global, 'R' for Rates, and 'A' for alpha emphasizing our goal to provide superior returns. I avoided using 'S' for swaps to remain focused on rates. This naming convention aligned with existing FX Concepts products like GCP and GFM. FXC embraced the idea.

Jim Conklin transferred Ross Bowser, Senior Research Analyst to the GRA Research Fixed Income Group, to program interest rate swaps and derive forward-starting interest rate swaps. He brought in Martin Hlusek from Prague as a Research Consultant-programmer, aiming for a full-time role, and he recruited Brett Holleman, a former colleague from Fortress, as the interest rate swaps trader for the GRA program. By the end of October, the team was fully staffed.

I created a GRA-fixed income marketing outline before talking to the team about models so that they would know what I was thinking. We were on the same page.

**Target Volatility:** GRA aimed for 8%, volatility matching the Bloomberg Barclays U.S. Aggregate Index, a key fixed income bond benchmark.

**Portfolio Focus:** GRA concentrated on the most liquid part of the yield curve, the first ten years, a prime maturity range of fixed income investors.

**Yield Curve Segmentation:** The GRA yield curve was divided into six discrete forward buckets: **1yr, 2yr, 3yr, 5yr, 7yr, 10yr**. Our marketing book highlighted the first four: The terminology is a little tricky—the points on the yield curve of the currencies are listed on the bottom of our marketing page (I copied them for readability):

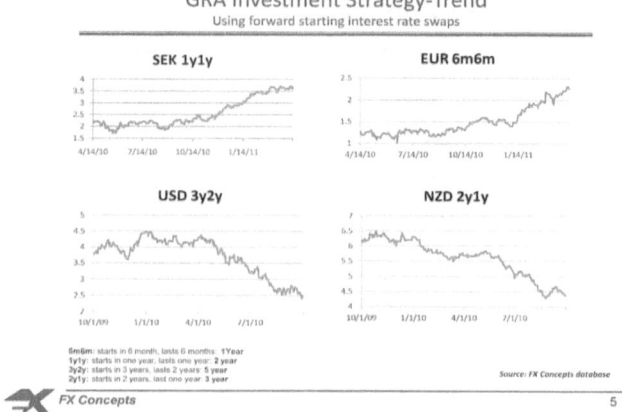

**SEK** (Swedish Krona)—**1y1y: starts in one year, lasts one year–2 years**

**EUR** (European Union) —**6m6m: starts in 6 months, lasts 6 months–1 year**

**USD** (US Dollar) —**3y2y: starts in 3 years, lasts 2 years– 5 years**

**NZD** (New Zealand Dollar)—**2y1y starts in 2 years, lasts one year–3 years**

FX Concepts traded thirty currencies, so it was suggested that the GRA program include as many rates as possible. My initial plan focused on the Group of Seven (G7) currencies, which actually comprised five main currencies. Due to recent news on the EURO, I aimed to start with these G7 currencies and use my research material from EAI for our marketing book. Consensus eventually settled on nine currencies, but we began with seven (the nine currencies are listed in the appendix).

During my monthly visits to NYC from California, Martin would fly in from Prague for the same week. With Ross, we closely collaborated on derivative programming and marketing efforts. While they focused on programming, I handled outreach to potential investors discussing progress and strategizing daily.

Martin and I were committed to fostering camaraderie within the FXC Research team, joining team lunches and meetings during our visit to NYC, and to contributing to a cohesive atmosphere. One day in August, when the FXC New York office building lost power and almost immediately started to warm up, Martin and I called in to mention we both shut off our air conditioners in solidarity. Our colleagues at FXC Research team made a deliberate effort to include us in their discussions and activities, enhancing team cohesion.

Team GRA aimed to start trading by January 1 to have a full year of performance data. To trade swaps, we needed an ISDA (International Swaps and Derivatives Association) agreement. ISDA agreements are typically used in over-the-counter derivative transactions to outline terms and conditions, including various events during a trade's lifespan.

Feeling impatient with the timing, I contacted my friend John Flint at Credit Suisse. Despite initial reluctance, John managed to persuade a credit representative at Credit Suisse to proceed with an ISDA agreement. The representative's interest piqued when they noticed our (FXC's) claim of twenty years' experience in Principal Component Analysis (PCA) with Relative Value, leading to the agreement's initiation.

Despite my prompt communication, FX Concepts just committed to working with Deutsche Bank, which allowed the GRA program to start trading a $19 million portfolio in January 2010.

Our GRA marketing book showcased FX Concepts' global presence, including offices in New York, London, Singapore, and Australia as well as a research office in Prague. Martin Hlusek operated at his home in at Pod Novym Lesem 52, Prague 6.

Within just three months, GRA emerged as a new fixed income strategy within the world's largest privately owned currency firm. However, we faced the challenge of starting with just $19 million.

I embarked on a trial run of our program with friends armed with the marketing book. A neighbor and friend, Jack Treynor, President of Treynor Capital, reviewed my GRA marketing presentation. He suggested focusing on fewer yield curve points and starting with G7 currencies, expanding gradually for better scalability and risk management. Jack asked if Western Asset traded forward-starting interest rate swaps, to which I confirmed they did not.

Jack's suggestion to reach out to large bond firms struck a chord with me, although I was skeptical about their willingness to outsource swaps management or adopt ideas from our FXC group. Instead, I felt that Martin and I should have been on road trips across the U.S. and London, targeting smaller quant fixed income and equity firms. We could have offered them the opportunity to integrate a quant fixed income program without the overhead of hiring additional staff. While it was not a missed opportunity, I believed we could revisit this strategy after demonstrating performance and fund growth.

Despite our intentions, Jim Conklin, Martin, and I never had the opportunity to present our GRA product together during our visit to NYC. FXC's marketing and management were preoccupied with addressing concerns about weak currency performance of the GCP.

By June 2010, the new GRA program yielded a net return of 9%. Meanwhile, according to the August 11, 2010, issue of Hedge Fund Alert, "FX Concepts Rebounds From 2009 losses: Through the end of July, FX Concepts GCP was up an average of 12% for 2010."

I scheduled a meeting with a former investor in FXC and my Western Asset hedge fund. Despite initially planning to trade in nine currencies with our GRA program, we focused on four due to market opportunities, rather than liquidity concerns. The prospect's persistent inquiries about forward swaps liquidity led me to end the meeting until I could address their concerns satisfactorily.

In my pursuit of data for our GRA swaps program, I reached out to the European Central Bank (ECB) based in Frankfurt, Germany. I identified myself as a researcher from FX Concepts, the world's largest currency manager, who was seeking the latest information on interest rate swaps and forward-starting interest rate swap liquidity globally. To my surprise, the ECB graciously shared insights from a recently completed study, providing us with the most up-to-date swaps information available. Armed with this valuable resource, I launched a campaign and informed prospects about our GRA swaps program, with an emphasis on the significance of the ECB's study's findings on swaps liquidity.

Given my focus on global initiatives, London seemed like an ideal market for our GRA program, especially considering the city's expertise in global fixed income. I started reaching out to schedule meetings in October, aligning with FX Concepts founder John Taylor's conference appearance. With GRA's impressive performance, boasting 14.82% net return by August, I dedicated myself to securing appointments every day.

Despite my busy schedule in London, I encountered disappointment as prospects questioned the absence of funding from a major FX Concepts client. To them, a $100 million derivative allocation for a fixed income assignment from larger firms seemed insignificant.

I hit all the big London firms that I met with on my Hollywood tour in 1994, and my speaker/manager tours 1995 and 1998. I met with senior people and staff.

I was pleased with the reception of the new product but just frustrated that nobody would take a step up. I was surprised that there was another firm, a London bond firm marketing a similar program, using five currencies and only three buckets—one, two, and three years. I kept hearing "come back when you have a fund open and $500 million in the fund".

One investor, a friend, said, "Pick an FX Concepts large investor, sit in their office until you have a deal, be aggressive with a founder's management fee, agree to manage the program for free for one year." He also asked why I had not gone to Switzerland where FX Concepts founder, CEO, CIO John Taylor had an office and was well known. It was a long flight home.

GRA performance took a dive at the end of 2010 ending at 7.08% net.

In 2011, we made "too many wrong mistakes," to quote Yogi Berra. Our GRA performance in January 2011 dipped to -1.59%. The sluggish response of our models to market changes was a major issue. To address this, Martin Hlusek took over swaps programming, from Jim. Despite Martin and Ross's efforts, our swaps trading remained costly, with most losses due to transactions costs. I later discovered that FXC management , not Martin or the technology, controlled the swaps selection and execution timing.

On February 4, 2011, after a workout at a 24-Hour Fitness gym near my FXC office in Long Beach, California, I suddenly experienced symptoms that made me fear I was having a heart attack. Lorraine rushed me to Torrance Hospital. Amidst the stress of the GRA program that weighed heavily on my mind, I could not help but worry about the outcome of Super Bowl XLV, where the Green Bay Packers were up against the Pittsburgh Steelers at

Cowboys Stadium in Arlington, Texas. Fortunately, the Packers emerged victorious, bringing some relief amidst the tumult.

After spending Friday night and all of Saturday in the hospital, I was discharged very late on Saturday night with strict instructions to head straight to bed. The doctors diagnosed it as a stress attack. I never told anyone at FX Concepts I was in the hospital.

On April 1, 2011, we launched our Global Rates Alpha Fund with $5 million, with Deutsche Bank as our Prime Broker. Despite challenges, our GRA Fund demonstrated positive performance in the first quarter of 2011. I marketed the $5 million Fund while knowing I needed to reach $100 million for any growth. I reached out to equity quant shops to gauge their interest in a fixed income quant program without additional hires. This approach received some positive feedback, which opened up new avenues for exploration.

The ongoing decline in FX Concepts' Global Currency Performance (GCP) throughout 2011 hindered my efforts to approach larger clients to seed a GRA program. FXC firm's AUM dropped from $8 billion when I joined in October of 2009 to $3 billion in 2011.

In July 2011, I received a call from Jim Conklin at home, informing me of his departure from FX Concepts. He did not provide a reason, but simply expressed his gratitude and apologized for the outcome.

Over Labor Day weekend in September 2011, Martin and I traveled to NYC for the FX Concepts Partners meeting. During the gathering, FX Concepts management announced the closure of the GRA program, citing distraction from fixed income and insufficient focus on currency as the reasons. FX Concepts honored my two-year contract. Martin and I stayed in NYC for the rest of the week.

Martin had a vision for the next chapter beyond FX Concepts and had been in discussions with his former colleague Jonathan Ratcliffe about launching a new venture. Their partnership dates back to London in 2004, where they collaborated on Relative Value (RV) derivative models. Jonathan Ratcliffe also shared a prior connection with Jim Conklin from their time at Fortress. Martin and I agreed to maintain communication via Skype. From September to November, Martin focused on rewriting all the models—Trend, Carry, and RV—and assessed their efficacy for their future endeavor.

## 21

## PRAGUE SIX

Jonathan Ratcliffe and I arranged to meet Martin Hlusek in Prague at the end of January to the first week in February 2012. Coincidently, Ross Bowser from FX Concepts was scheduled to be in Prague for vacation during that period. He intended to join Martin for an Iron Man marathon. Martin, Ross, and Jonathan shared a passion for triathlons. Jonathan lived in London, so it was an easy flight, less than two hours, down to Prague.

During one of our Skype sessions in December, Martin and Jonathan surprised me with the announcement of their newly co-founded venture, **Prague Six Asset Management**. They even had business cards printed. Their emphasis on ownership stemmed from past disappointments with previous owners—Jonathan's ordeal at Harness and Martin's struggle for execution authority at FX Concepts were compelling factors. I felt unsettled by this development, but my options were limited. I was offered the COO title with responsibilities spanning marketing, client service, and more, all without a fixed salary—just 35% commission on my contributions. My objective was to familiarize myself with PowerPoint and any available IT programs. Nothing was formalized in writing.

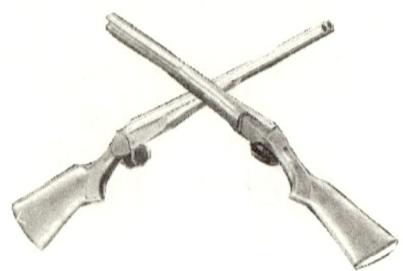

Martin and Jonathan crafted a striking marketing book for Prague Six Asset Management's fixed income forward-starting swaps program. The cover featured two crossed shotguns with the bold declaration, "Our program will blow you away!" This imagery was inspired by Jonathan's residence on an estate north of London, where he and Martin often enjoyed hunting together. The inclusion of shotguns on the cover was a nod to their shared experiences and interests.

Martin and Jonathan combined the best ideas from our GRA book and Jonathan's fixed income derivative marketing materials in a meticulously detailed presentation. Jonathan promised to bring samples of the book to Prague to showcase their collaborative effort. Additionally, Jonathan was enhancing our website to ensure a polished online presence. Upon our arrival in Prague, Jonathan distributed our business cards, thereby further solidifying our professional image.

Timothy O'Grady

Prague Six Asset Management
Pod Novym Lesem 52
Prague 6

T + 1 626 833 9560
E timothy.ogrady@praguesix.com

The Z sign in front of Prague Six is the lowercase of the Greek letter Zeta; the sixth letter of the Greek alphabet. It denotes the so-called Riemann function, which has a simple definition but an unsolved (unproven) hypothesis stated by Riemann in 1859. This hypothesis remains one of the most intriguing mysteries in the world of prime numbers.

Positioning Prague Six adds a layer of distinction to our identity. In Eastern Europe, Prague Six carries significant prestige, making it a sought-after location. Our goal was to differentiate ourselves from the typical London 'quant firm' archetype. We saw Prague as the emerging nucleus of the investment world, and we were eager to attract Euro and Eastern European investors seeking promising opportunities. Additionally, Martin's residence in Prague Six further anchored our presence and commitment to the area.

In the summer of 2010, Lorraine and I found ourselves on a Danube Boat Cruise from Prague to Budapest. Our journey, however, did not start as smoothly as we'd hoped. A delayed flight out of LAX delayed our arrival in Prague. Determined not to miss our dinner, I made a bold move and convinced a limo driver to take us all the way up the hill to the National Museum at the top of Wenceslas Square. Despite the roped-off area, the driver managed to navigate through and drop us off right at the front gate. In hindsight, I might have been a bit generous with the tip in Czech Krona! We joined our tour dinner group just as they were eating dessert, which made for a memorable start to our vacation.

In 2010, Martin's absence in Prague did not deter him from

extending a thoughtful gesture to us. While he was vacationing in Spain, he generously gifted Lorraine and me tickets to a private concert featuring Beethoven and Mozart at the Municipal House. Our Danube Boat Tour Group was impressed that I was able to get tickets to such an exclusive concert which had been sold out for weeks.

Thanks to accumulated airline miles from my FX Concepts marketing travels, my trip to Prague in February 2012 turned out to be virtually cost-free. Martin found reasonably priced hotels along the tram line by taking advantage of the offseason when rooms were plentiful and rates more affordable. During my stay, I lodged at the Hotel Savoy on Keplerova Street, conveniently situated near Prague Castle, and the Pohorelec stop on tram line 22.

On Saturday, February 4, 2012, my journey from LAX to Prague via London Heathrow hit a snag when a rare snowstorm forced Heathrow to close. We learned of the closure mid-flight and were initially diverted to Paris. However, Paris-Charles de Gaulle was full and closed too, so we ended up back at Heathrow.

At London Heathrow, I found a seat and bought some food while waiting. The internet was down, so I called Lorraine who promptly e-mailed Martin and Jonathan, "Tim just called from London/Heathrow. His flight to Prague was canceled, and he got a booking on BA #0858, leaving Heathrow at 19:05. His computer/WIFI was not working, so he phoned me. I hope you can look up his arrival time and still meet him. Thanks." Martin confirmed he would meet me at Prague airport.

Upon arrival in Prague, I was one of three passengers who disembarked the plane at Prague without luggage. While others seemed to have resigned to the luggage situation, I was the visibly upset. My luggage had gone on an impromptu vacation to Greece and Turkey and arrived four days later. With the help of the hotel staff who were fluent in multiple languages, I coordinated with the airlines to retrieve my belongings.

On Monday morning, I was still in the clothes I had arrived in, except for fresh underwear and socks—clothes my wife insisted I pack with my carry-on bag. Ross lent me a few more pairs. After breakfast at the hotel, I took the Tram from the green metro line to the National Technical Library, using Czech koruna to buy the ticket.

Our Prague Six business meetings took place at the National Technical Library near the Dejvicka station. Martin, a Prague resident, often used the Library for his Ph.D. work. This was my first in-person meeting with Jonathan, although we had spoken on Skype before. In the photo, Martin Hlusek is seated on the left, I am at the back left, facing the camera and taking notes. Jonathan Ratcliffe is in the center/front, reviewing models. In the back right, you can see Ross, who had just joined us after his workout.

After lunch, Jonathan requested a one-on-one with me, so we went to a separate room. Since we were all still getting to know each other, he wanted to assess how quickly I could secure a substantial investment—a hundred yards. In currency terms, 'a hundred yards' means $100 million. He inquired about my fundraising track record at FX Concepts. I informed that I had raised $24 million in a year and a half.

I presented a detailed business plan outlining our target clients, estimated assets under management (AUM), and projected timelines. Jonathan emphasized the urgency of securing $100 million by June, which highlighted his financial obligations and need for immediate action. Our company was named, the marketing materials were finalized, and the website was nearly completed—all that remained was to secure client cash flow.

I met with several equity quant shops and there was interest in adding a quant derivative fixed income program to complement their existing quant equity programs. The target firms lacked the fixed income derivative skills and were open to outsourcing the forward-starting interest rate swaps program to Prague Six.

Initially, Martin would need to be on their trading desks to establish a comfort level with our recommendations, utilizing the firms' ISDAs. I had several prime brokers working with me, but Jonathan was not impressed. He ended the meeting abruptly and walked out to tell Martin we had a problem: Tim could not bring in any money right away.

*Shark Tank*, the TV show that supports startups, might have been the path for Prague Six if I had been aware of its existence. With my TV and movie connections, I would have approached *Shark Tank* without hesitation. Kevin O'Leary's keen interest in cryptocurrencies could have made us stand out. Also, Sir Richard Branson's presence, whose journey began in a church crypt, might have added intrigue.

Dinner that night was pleasant, although I found myself observing rather than engaging in conversation. I opted for a famous Czech beer, Bernhard's, reminiscent of gathering with a Czech neighbor back in California. I made a mental note to bring back a few sixpacks as souvenirs. Surprisingly, my knowledge of Bernhard's beer seemed to impress the Prague Six team.

Our routine persisted as we convened at the Library daily to meticulously document everything, ensuring we were all on the same page. Managing operations from three different locations (California, Prague, London) presented its own challenges, but we remained committed to overcoming them. Each evening, we sought solace in the warmth of a nearby pub, indulging in hearty meals and enjoying the crisp taste of Bernhard's beer. These moments provided much-needed relaxation and camaraderie, allowing us to unwind after the day's work.

One night, three days after my arrival, Martin, Ross, Jonathan, and I found ourselves at the Cigar Bar on Dlouha Street, aptly named for its length. While I was on the phone with hotel staff, I received some good news—my missing suitcase had been located. However, there was a catch: I needed to rush to Prague airport to claim it, but first, I had to prove my identity. With cigars and brandy snifters in tow, we stepped outside to await a tram. I distinctly remember the biting cold; temperatures dropped to a bone chilling -20C (-4 degrees Fahrenheit). As we waited for tram #26, a limo adorned with an advertisement for a strip club caught our attention. Because of the freezing weather, Jonathan, who was shivering uncontrollably, humorously exclaimed, "Give me the fattest girl so I can give her a big hug." Eventually, we reached the airport, where I successfully proved my identity and retrieved my luggage.

At the end of the week, we decided to continue our collaboration remotely. Jonathan would operate from London, Martin from Prague, and me from California. We agreed to use Dropbox for document sharing and committed to weekly Skype meetings to stay in sync. Despite our efforts, Prague Six ever launched operations. On March 12, 2012, I officially left Prague Six to join my son at ROW Asset Management.

# 22

# ROW ASSET MANAGEMENT

When my son Ryan offered me a role at his new company, ROW Asset Management (ROWAM) in Newport Beach, CA—I accepted. As the name Commodity Trading Advisor (CTA) suggests, ROW specialized in commodities trading. With my FINRA **Series 3** License from my time at EAI, I ventured into new territory with confidence, ready to innovate and adapt.

I joined the team on March 12, 2012, when ROW comprised a modest group of six employees-four pictured from FX Trader Magazine April-June 2014: Seng Ung, me, FXC colleagues and co-founders Jeffrey Weiser and Ryan O'Grady. Debra Oaks and Janessa Garcia Scudder not pictured.

Operating from a single office located in Newport Beach, CA, with $13 million in assets under management (AUM), we faced the challenge of establishing ourselves as a new firm 3,000 miles away from New York. Despite the distance, we were fully staffed and motivated, although we encountered challenges with our prime broker.

Securing meetings with prospects who were willing to meet exclusively outside their office posed a notable challenge. It is often a red flag, particularly when pension investors or consultants suggest meeting at a nearby Starbucks. Meetings held in a consultant's office usually triggered formal documentation in their manager database, followed by additional research by designated personnel. The choice of meeting environment significantly influenced the perceived level of seriousness and the subsequent outcomes of these interactions. Nonetheless, I recognized the importance of starting somewhere, and I appreciated that they took my call at least.

Ryan's academic achievements and early career accomplishments were truly impressive. His perfect 800 score on the math section of the college SATs highlighted his exceptional quantitative abilities from a young age. During his pursuit of an economics degree at Johns Hopkins University, Ryan seized an opportunity for a summer internship at Neuberger Berman, a prestigious fixed income manager in New York City.

During his internship, Ryan's innovative spirit shone brightly as he developed a fixed income trend trading model. This model was based on a moving average crossover of three U.S. Treasury prices and showcased his ability to apply theoretical concepts in practice settings. Ryan's outstanding performance during his internship earned him an invitation to return the following summer. This ultimately brought him to the attention of FX Concepts through Neuberger's connections. Remarkably, Ryan was only seventeen years old when Neuberger expressed interest in him. Upon learning his age, Theresa Havel, the founder, and co-head of Neuberger's Fixed Income Group reached out to me at EAI for clarification. I suggested that Neuberger Berman hire him as a consultant until he turned eighteen years old, a recommendation they promptly acted on by hiring Ryan.

The O'Grady family's foray into computing began in 1983 with Lorraine's purchase of the Franklin Ace 1200, an Apple II clone. Lorraine made this decision to embrace technology, opting for the Franklin Ace 1200, with its 8 KB of RAM and 16 KB of ROM and a 5 ¼" floppy drive—an impressive setup at the time. The price tag of around $2200 represented a substantial financial investment to have technology in our home. Pictured below is a Franklin Ace 1200 with game controller.

# THE EXCEPTIONAL LIFE OF AN ORDINARY MAN 205

Within a year of acquiring the Franklin Ace 1200, Lorraine and I enrolled in a beginner programming class taught at Mattatuck Community College, a local institution. Guided by our instructor, who was also an algebra teacher, we embarked on our programming journey. Our first task in class was to solve the quadric equation, a fundamental exercise in mathematics. Our instructor reminded us that A cannot equal zero and X yields two answers. Since I struggled to find X when there was only one answer, I made the decision to seek someone to hire who could find X for me.

$$ax^2 + bx + c = 0$$
$$x = \frac{-b \pm \sqrt{b^2 - 4ac}}{2a}$$

At ROW, my focus was marketing a new program—ROW Diversified, a global macro program spanning interest rates, currencies, energy, equities, and commodities.

In the last week of March 2012, Ryan was a speaker at a Battle of the Quants conference at the Union Club in New York City. Jeff Weiser, ROW President, and I thought it would be a good time to introduce ROW Diversified with a press release while Ryan and Jeff were at the conference.

As the Battle of the Quants conference wrapped up, Ryan's call about John Smith's interest in meeting with ROW ignited excitement. John Smith, renowned as Head of Trading and Quantitative Allocations, Senior Portfolio Manager at UBS Alternative and Quantitative Investments in Stamford, CT, was a top prospect on any quant marketing list. With no designated rooms for speaker/attendee meetings at the Union Club, Ryan, Jeff, and John converged in a hallway.

Despite spending six years nurturing these connections, we never finalized an investment deal with UBS. ROW Diversified made it onto UBS finals twice, but we ultimately fell short of securing an investment. Interestingly, my two largest investors in the Western Asset hedge fund were UBS and Blackstone, each at $150 million, capped at $150 million each. Despite coming close with UBS, my efforts, including facilitating a lucrative currency options trade in the Western Asset Credit Protection Fund for Blackstone, failed to elicit a return phone call from them.

Creating marketing materials for a new product has always been an enjoyable and enlightening process for me, which has offered valuable teaching moments along the way. However, this time around, I knew it would present a unique challenge.

ROW's diversified investment portfolio included an array of futures contracts, spanning various asset classes:

- 11 global equity indices
- 7 energy contracts
- 7 agricultural product contracts
- 8 softs/livestock contracts
- 5 metals contracts
- 28 currency forwards

Systematic managers maintain no long bias; they remain agnostic to market direction; therefore, all futures/forward positions can be long or short. This flexibility is a fundamental aspect of our strategy and enables us to adapt to changing market conditions and capitalize on opportunities regardless of market direction.

ROW's managed futures management stands out with its innovative expansion of the tradable universe. Pioneering synthetic assets known as clusters, ROW generates thousands daily, enhancing portfolio flexibility and diversification.

Initially clusters were simple, with four assets per cluster, categorized by currencies, equities, and commodities. Constraints ensured clusters remained within their respective classes, but recent advancements removed these limitations, which allowed for greater flexibility. Proprietary technology leveraging Principal Component Analysis (PCA) determines position weights within each cluster to ensure an optimal allocation of capital.

All portfolio trades were overseen by portfolio manager, Jeffrey Weiser, who boasts twenty-five years of experience trading in various market conditions. Since he started, Jeffrey has been the best emerging market currency trader in the business.

While I grasped the main performance engines of the global macro strategy, Trend, RV & Mean Reversion and Carry, I lacked understanding of the programming behind the models. I recognized this gap and realized that my best chance for success at ROWAM would be to pursue prospects to meet Ryan. He could effectively explain the systematic process and the intricate models that drive our strategy.

Ryan and Seng played instrumental roles in creating slides and exhibits outlining Trend, RV, and Carry strategies across various asset classes, including currencies, rates, energy, equities, and commodities. They also ensured that these exhibits were aligned to demonstrate effective risk control.

During presentations, Ryan often utilized a whiteboard to illustrate how a particular strategy would respond to changes in the market. He would provide a general outline before zooming in on specific questions raised by the prospects to ensure a tailored and insightful discussion.

During my tenure of nine years at ROW, the company expanded its research capabilities by adding two full-time Research employees in Newport Beach—both UCLA MFA graduates: Gurunath Dasari and John Yu joined UCLA MFA graduate Seng Ung. Ryan was instrumental as one of the founding members of the Industry Advisory Board (IAB) for the UCLA Anderson School of

Management Master's in Financial Engineering (MFE) Program. As a board member, Ryan actively recruited potential research candidates, offering students paid summer internships to assess their suitability for a permanent position.

Despite the presence of great, intelligent young minds, my limited math skills often left me feeling out of my depth. I relied heavily on Seng whenever ROW made model changes. There were times when I voiced frustration to Seng if the models behaved differently than expected, even if I was mistaken. Nevertheless, I valued Seng's expertise and support in navigating the complexities of our models.

I ensured prospects could access ROW Currency and ROW Diversified performance across various hedge fund databases to maximize visibility. However, managing databases became challenging, especially in supplying monthly information, as many were designed for long-only equity and bond positions and struggled to adapt to alternative positions like futures. Timers for inputting data and discrepancies in asset group definitions complicated matters. Despite these challenges, I expanded databases beyond ROW's initial setup. Ultimately, Janessa volunteered to assist in navigating the programs. I wanted to ensure that prospects seeking information on ROW Asset Management's programs could easily locate us.

I had the opportunity to secure meetings for ROW at the June Chicago MFA conference. Mike Boss of Newedge, a Chicago capital introduction firm, invited Jeff, Ryan, and me to lunch at his club rather than at the conference. This meeting was significant as it led to collaboration with Newedge/Société Générale's capital introduction team—Mike Boss, Ryan Duncan, Chris Kennedy, and Matt McCarthy—over the next few years on hedge fund prospect meetings. More details on Newedge to follow.

At my inaugural Chicago MFA conference in June 2012, I arranged a meeting with Jerrett Yelton, a senior analyst at SSARIS in Wilton, Connecticut. Pursuing SSARIS for months, I believed

ROW Diversified aligned well with their programs. We scheduled the last time slot, on the final day of the conference. Before the SSARIS meeting, I had a prior engagement with Efficient Capital Management. To accommodate, ROW managed to secure a vacant room after organizers began dismantling the temporary walls of the managers' meeting room.

For the SSARIS meeting, Jarrett brought Carlos Cabrera, an asset allocator from Jefferies Bache. With no available meeting rooms, Carlos suggested relocating to the bar. There, Jeff and Carlos enjoyed a glass of wine, but I declined, feeling frustrated. The meeting progressed positively until the topic of options arose. Carlos said 'his guy' did not like options, suggesting their removal from the portfolio mix, but Ryan advocated for their retention. We agreed to revisit the topic later. As we exited the bar, we debated options in the Diversified program en route to the airport. Despite differing opinions, Ryan remained steadfast: options would stay.

I convinced ROW to sponsor an Opal Public Funds conference in Las Vegas in October 2012. One of the benefits of being a sponsor was that Ryan would be a speaker. During the event, I ensured to introduce myself and ROW funds to Wilshire, the main consultant speaker. Wilshire's presentation focused on emerging managers and the smaller managers' tendency to outperform larger ones.

Wilshire's criteria for emerging managers, which required at least $1 billion AUM, sparked discussion. However, they maintained this threshold, thereby limiting visibility for smaller managers. Other consultants like Callan and Mercer set higher AUM thresholds ($10 billion and $20 billion, respectively). Despite familiarity with ROW from their time at FX Concepts interest from these consultants was minimal until ROW programs reached larger AUM sizes. At EAI Consulting, we presented exceptional managers regardless of AUM, leveraging support from EAI consultants.

Rob Lingle from Asset Alliance Advisors rented space in the

ROW office complex. Rob's office was equipped with a Bloomberg terminal. I was able to use the terminal to access Bloomberg Mandates, a service that listed hedge fund opportunities. I became a top user of LinkedIn, Preqin, and Bloomberg Mandates compiling lists of potential searches and reaching out to prospects via phone and email.

In January 2013, Miami hosted two concurrent hedge fund conferences: the MFA Forum, followed in the same week by Context Summits. Although scheduled for Context Summits, ROW Asset Management received a surprise invitation from Carlos Cabrera to attend the MFA Forum. Representing Jefferies, Carlos offered the invitation due to extra slots available as they were a sponsor. Accepting the offer, I planned to join Ryan and Jeff at Concepts Summits later that week.

At the MFA Forum I pitched to Oliver Alliker, CIO of Scout Global Funds, of Ultimo, NSW Australia. Scout, an early-stage investor in emerging managers via managed accounts, was interested in systematic trading expertise. ROW's systematic global macro approach was an ideal fit. Carlos Cabrera unexpectedly joined our meeting and delivered the impressive ROW presentation. Oliver agreed to meet with Ryan for a ROW Diversified managed account investment. Carlos also reminded me that he would pick me up for Jefferies' dinner that night.

Carlos facilitated my registration for the Powers Sessions MFA Forum, where I engaged with key investors like Alkesh Gianchandani of Deutsche Bank. I pitched the ROW Diversified program for inclusion on Deutsche Bank's global platform, db Select. During dinner, I presented to Ally Damree of Superfund, who expressed interest in emerging manager opportunities. Leveraging my connection with Martin Hlusek, my former Prague Six partner, I sought information on Superfund in Vienna before initiating correspondence with Ally Damree.

In 2013, ROW expanded its footprint to NYC by bringing on

board Laurie Pisano from FX Concepts in March. Jeff's desire to return to NYC played a role, and with FX Concepts closing in September, Ryan seized the opportunity to recruit Saurabh Kumar as Research Director. With Saurabh and Laurie joining the team, Ryan, Debra Oaks and Jeff reunited their original 2001 Global Currency Program (GCP) team.

In 2013, I introduced Ryan to Pacific Alternative Asset Management Company (PAMCO) located near ROW Asset Management in Irvine, CA. I had a prior connection with Jane Buchan, founder, CIO, dating back to her time at Collins & Co in 1994. Jane and Sam Dietrich from PAAMCO had invested in the Western Asset San Gabriel Opportunity Fund in 2002. I had also pitched Jane when I was at FX Concepts.

Ryan introduced the ROW Diversified Fund to Jane, Sam, and their team at PAAMCO. Typically, inquiries about management and incentive fees signal interest, but PAAMCO's focus on lower hedge fund fees made it more of a routine question than a genuine expression of interest.

Out of the blue, PAAMCO's Sam Dietrich called, remembering Ryan's success at FX Concepts managing multi-billion currency assignments. His excited inquiry as to whether ROW still handled currency revealed an order he was eager to confirm. I waved at Ryan, and he took the call-in which Sam explained the opportunity. The client, a group of Wall Street executives, sought experienced hedge fund managers after failing to manage their assets independently. ROW's $35 million AUM in combination with the $50 million from this investor group, qualified ROW as a QPAM, a prerequisite for the assignment. Ryan sealed the deal.

ROW Asset Management's ROW Diversified program's remarkable performance of **+3.78% in May 2013** elevated the firm's reputation virtually overnight. Amidst market turmoil where most funds suffered losses, ROW Diversified stood out. The taper tantrum, sparked by fears of the Federal Reserve's scaling back of quantitative easing, further underscored the significance of ROW's achievement. As inquiries flooded in, I reassured prospects that performance was accurate and encouraged them to speak directly with Ryan for further clarification. This pivotal moment marked ROW's emergence as a standout performer in a turbulent market, highlighting the value of ROW Diversified as a strategic addition to investor portfolios. I diligently contacted every prospect on our lists and ensured that our information was updated across various databases.

In 2014, while our clients were in managed accounts, the ROW Diversified Fund still relied solely on Ryan's initial investment. My focus shifted to gaining exposure for the fund in national hedge fund publications. A feature about Ryan and ROW Asset Management in Barclayhedge caught my attention and led to connections with their team in Iowa. Although I was not involved in the article, I pursued getting the ROW Diversified Fund listed on Barclayhedge's monthly manager performance list. Despite having over $100 million in the strategy but only $13 million in the fund, Barclayhedge agreed to list the ROW Diversified Strategy (not fund) in their monthly listings.

I successfully expanded efforts to list the ROW Diversified Strategy on various databases including Bloomberg, where it was listed with the ticker ROWDIV. Subsequently, I ensured that our ROW Diversified 2X Fund with ticker ROWDXF and our ROW Relative Value Fund ticker ROWFVR were added to Bloomberg when the Funds were launched.

We established a connection with ADMIS Diversified Strategies Fund, overseen by Emanuel Balarie and Jack Schwager (renowned author of the *Market Wizards* series). They initially invested $2 million with ROW Diversified in a managed account but further asset growth for investment was not achieved.

In January/February 2014, ROW participated in numerous meetings at MFA and at Context. Despite my extensive efforts via calls and emails, we did not secure any major deals.

To accelerate asset gathering, Ryan and Jeff consulted with Bruce Wilson of North Creek Advisors who were known for expediting AUM growth. I engaged with North Creek salespeople, sharing my contact lists and prioritizing prospects. I said my next call was my #1 prospect.

The North Creek team reached out to their contacts at UBS, Blackstone, Mercer, and other key prospects. At the end of 2014, ROW Diversified had achieved an impressive performance of 27.11% net of all fees.

With the ROW Diversified success behind us, I became exceptionally aggressive in securing meetings at the January 2015 MFA Forum and Context in Miami. I was constantly in touch with Mike Boss of Newedge Société Générale; we prioritized prospects and secured a crucial meeting with Abu Dhabi, facilitated by Matt McCarthy. Despite BlackRock's request for an hour of our time, I scheduled twenty-nine meetings from Monday to Wednesday noon at the MFA Forum.

At Context on Thursday and Friday, I scheduled thirty-four meetings; Jeff insisted I reduce it to that number. The ROW schedule on Thursday started at 8:00 a.m., with the only break all day from 10:00 to 10:30. Ryan took the floor by himself until 10:00 a.m. to accommodate Jeff's trading activities, then Jeff joined the meetings. Ryan took a break when Jeff arrived.

On Thursday, the investment firm FRM joined Smith-Pamplona Capital at 10:30 to open a half-hour slot for Ryan. Friday's schedule started at 8:00 a.m., with a break again at 10:30 due to a canceled meeting. Two meetings between 2:30 to 3:30 p.m. were axed to accommodate LGT from Zurich at 5:00 to 6:00 pm. I made sure they had an hour break in the afternoon. Ryan and Jeff skipped breakfast and there was no time for lunch. Despite my efforts, some prospects remained elusive. Matt McCarthy of Newedge Société Générale stepped in to assist with a 3:30 p.m. meeting on Friday to help me with a prospect from a large west pension plan. Matt volunteered to make sure the prospect got the best Société Générale treatment before the meeting. Overall, Ryan felt optimistic about several prospects after MFA and Context.

In March 2015, ROW Diversified clinched the title for the best three-year performance, earning the prestigious 2014 'Systematic Emerging Global Macro Manager of the Year Award'. Jeff and Debra represented ROW at a dinner in NYC, where they graciously accepted the award.

I was not surprised at the award. I was waiting for the June 2015 Chicago Managed Futures Pinnacle Awards that are handed out at the first night dinner at the MFA conference. ROW Diversified did not win the 'Best Managed Futures-Systematic Global Macro-three-year Performance Award'. I was shocked, then angry. I called Sol Waksman, President of Barclayhedge and demanded to know why ROW Diversified did not win. Sol explained that FORT LP was simply a better-known firm than ROW. I said they are a lot older and, naturally, they would be better known. Before I did anything stupid, I thanked Sol for his time and hung up. I always check to see where ROW Diversified performance is against FORT. Time for a vacation!

## 23

## CAMINO DE SANTIAGO
## "WAY OF ST. JAMES"

Lorraine and I had traveled throughout Europe on numerous occasions, but we had never visited Spain. To remedy this, Lorraine arranged for us to join the 'Across Spain and Portugal-Paradores and Pousadas' tour with Odysseys Unlimited. This tour featured unique accommodations, including Paradores in Spain and Pousadas in Portugal, known for their five-star quality and stunning locations in restored castles, monasteries, manor houses and palaces. It promised an unforgettable experience of history and luxury.

After enjoying the Northern Tour in 2015, which had taken us through Lisbon, Oporto, Santiago de Compostela, Bilbao, and Barcelona, we were eager to join the Southern Tour in 2016. This journey would take us from Lisbon to Seville, Cordoba, Ronda, and Madrid.

In high school, I took two years of Latin. I explored the language and the impressive engineering feats of ancient Rome, such as projects, roads, aqueducts, bridges, and walls constructed before the birth of Christ, yet still functional. Lorraine, on the other hand, had taken four years of Spanish in high school and an additional year her first year in college. Her Spanish skills proved invaluable during our travels.

Lorraine wrote her college thesis on 'The Effect of The Islamic Religion on Islamic Art', inspired by her travels throughout Turkey funded by a scholarship during the summer of her sophomore to junior class year. Her year-long research involved extensive reading, time in NYC libraries, and contact with authors and artists. The history and art of North African Muslims who conquered Spain and Portugal in AD 711 and ruled for 800 years added significant depth and meaning to our vacation.

In Barcelona, our 2015 trip concluded with days spent admiring the artwork of Gaudi, Miro, and Pablo Picasso. A highlight was dining at the same place as the Barcelona soccer team. Our waiter cleverly arranged for fans from our group to meet the team. Although I skipped meeting Lionel Messi, one the greatest soccer players of all time, I bought a Barcelona soccer shirt. Wearing it has sparked great conversations ever since.

Lisbon, Portugal, was the starting point for our trips across Spain. The Monument of Discoveries, located on the Tagus River, marks the place where Portuguese caravels set off to explore and colonize the world. It is easy to forget that Portugal dominated early global sea exploration in the 1400s with their small but mighty ships. By navigating along the African coast and then east across the Indian Ocean to Asia, Portuguese explorers achieved a historic feat: connecting Europe and Asia by an ocean route.

Having captured Constantinople (now Istanbul), the Ottoman Turks controlled vital trade routes, like the Bosporus Straits and the Mediterranean Sea, hindering land travel from Europe to Asia. This control gave Muslims a trade monopoly with India via land routes, such as the Silk Roads from China, along which they exchanged goods. Marco Polo was the first European to travel extensively in China and Asia and document his journeys.

In 1492, Christopher Columbus sought a western route to Asia, sponsored by King Ferdinand II and Queen Isabella I of Spain. Despite the prevailing belief that the earth was round, Columbus' estimate of its circumference was about 25% too small. He based his estimate on the work of Arab astronomers and assumed the Arabic mile used in the estimate was the same as the Italian mile, which was actually about 30% longer. Columbus also had help from Marco Polo's travel diaries to understand the people when he reached India. As always, there were rumors that Christopher Columbus knew the 'correct milage' but to sell the voyage and find a crew, he needed a shorter route. Good salesman—royalty paid for four voyages.

While traveling from Lisbon up to Porto along the Atlantic coast, we spotted pilgrims equipped with walking sticks, hats, shells, and backpacks following the 'Portuguese Way' to Santiago de Compostela. Their route was marked by yellow arrows and blue scallop shells. Our guide began to introduce us to the pilgrimage, also known as the Camino de Santiago, the Way of Saint James.

Santiago de Compostela, located in upper left corner of Spain (see image from Google Earth), owes its establishment to the pilgrimage to the tomb of Saint James. Prior to the Camino, this remote area in the northwest of Spain had no town.

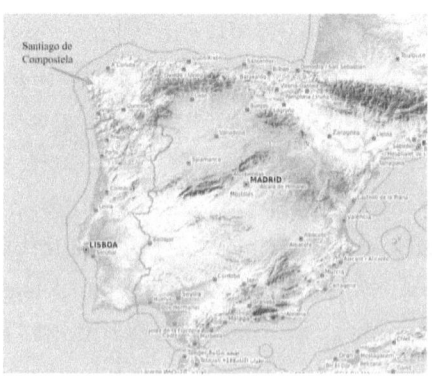

According to our tour guide Margarete, James the Greater, the brother of John, was one of the twelve apostles of Jesus as per the New Testament. After leaving his work as a fisherman in Galilee, he became one of Christ's earliest apostles. Despite traveling to the northwest of Spain (Galicia) during the early years of his brief ministry, James had limited success in gathering only a few disciples. Two of those disciples, Theodore and Athanasius, accompanied James back to Judea where James was beheaded by the order of Herod Agrippa in 44 AD, which made him the first disciple to be martyred.

Legend has it that after Saint James was beheaded, his disciples carried his body back to the coast of Galicia near a place where James had preached. He was buried there, and over time, his disciples were also laid to rest alongside him. The location of his tomb was forgotten for centuries.

The Spanish name 'Santiago' translates to James. 'Compostela' originates from the Latin 'campus stellae', meaning 'field of stars'. Legend has it that since the Middle Ages, pilgrims believed that the stars of the Milky Way were formed by the apostle St. James himself, guiding them to his tomb.

In the ninth century, shepherds allegedly observed mysterious celestial signs in the sky while tending their flocks. Guided by these heavenly clues, the Bishop of Iria Flavia, Teodomiro, discovered the tomb of the apostle James.

In another legend, Emperor Charlemagne dreams of Saint James the Greater during the Crusades against the Moors. James promises Charlemagne victory over the Moors in Spain and reveals a vision of a starry road to his tomb. Charlemagne's subsequent triumph victory in battle elevated both him and Saint James to international celebrity status.

Saint James' reputation as a miracle worker spread widely and drew pilgrims from across Europe to his tomb in Northwest Spain. Despite its remote location, pilgrims from Austria, Belgium, England, France, Germany, Italy, Luxembourg, the Netherlands, and Portugal embarked on their own Camino from their front doors, trekking across Spain to visit Saint James' tomb and to beg for his intercession.

After reaching Santiago, many pilgrims extended their journey to Finisterre (about 70 km further west on the Atlantic coast), which is believed to be the 'end of the earth', as 'finis' means 'end' and 'terre' means 'earth'. There, they collected shells abundant in the ocean as proof of their pilgrimage. The scallop shell symbolizes the various routes traveled by pilgrims worldwide, all converging at the tomb of Saint James in Santiago de Compostela.

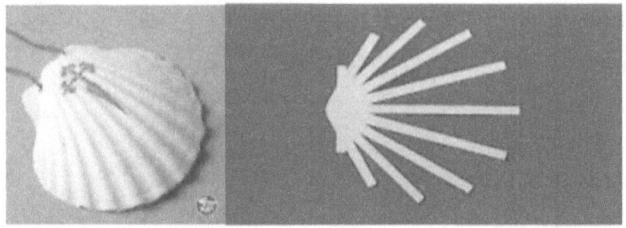

Our journey in Spain began at the Parador (Hostal de los Reyes Católicos) in Santiago de Compostela, built in 1499 as a hospital for pilgrims on the Camino de Santiago by King Ferdinand II and

Queen Isabella I. It reflected their religious devotion and efforts to enhance infrastructure and services along pilgrimage routes in Spain.

King Ferdinand II and Queen Isabella I built hostels, bridges, churches, and wells along the pilgrimage route, with their notable project being the hospital, Hostal de los Reyes Católicos, near Santiago Cathedral. This hospital provided free, round-the-clock medical and spiritual care for pilgrims, allowing them to recover for up to three days in the summer and five days in the winter. Santiago de Compostela, a pilgrimage site since the ninth century, ranked among the most visited destinations in the Middle Ages, after Jerusalem and Rome.

In the Middle Ages, pilgrims on the Camino de Compostela often faced physical challenges and threats from bandits. To protect them, the Order of Santiago—also known as the Order of Saint James—was established and resembled the Knights Templar. Unlike the Knights Templar, the Order of Santiago focused on protecting pilgrims within Spain, not the Holy Land. Our second Spanish Parador, Parador de Leon, was a monastery that had served as a residence for the Knights of the Order of Saint James.

The Cathedral of Santiago features a Holy Door (Porta Santa) on the Plaza Praza da Quintana. Passing through it during jubilee years grants believers a plenary indulgence, absolving them from sins. After passing through, pilgrims confess, receive the Holy Communion, recite the Creed, and offer prayers for the Pope and personal intentions. Through this ritual, believers are cleansed of sin, which paves their way to heaven without the need to go to purgatory.

The Holy Door of Santiago only opens during Compostelan

Holy Years, which occur when the feast of the Apostle Santiago (25 July) falls on a Sunday. The Holy door last opened in 2010 and was not scheduled to be open again until 2021. However, on March 13, 2015, Pope Francis announced an extraordinary jubilee, a Holy Year of Mercy lasting from December 8, 2015, until November 20, 2016. The jubilee year began with the opening of the Holy Door of Saint Peter's Basilica, followed by other Holy Doors of basilicas worldwide, symbolizing a pathway to grace and salvation to believers everywhere.

The next morning, Lorraine and I explored the Plaza de Obradoiro Square outside the Parador. The ancient flagstones, which have been smoothed by pilgrims over centuries, welcomed weary but exhilarated travelers. Upon arrival, pilgrims become part of an ancient and religious rite that has remained unchanged over eleven centuries. At church services later, we learned that 300,000 pilgrims from 130 nationalities completed the Camino the previous year, with each nationality's arrival celebrated during the service.

The decision to embark on our Camino came as a surprise to both of us. Our children and lifelong friends were surprised when we shared our plan. It was a spontaneous choice, one that simply felt right at that particular moment in our lives. Once we made the decision, we agreed to extend our vacation for this new adventure and to start our Camino the day after our 2016 Southern Spain trip ended.

## 24

## SIN-FREE

Inspired by the transformative journey depicted in the movie *The Way*, starring actor Martin Sheen and directed and by son Emilio Estevez, Lorraine and I embarked on preparations for our own Camino journey. We immersed ourselves in books about the Camino, scoured the web for gear recommendations, and experimented with various clothing, footwear, and hiking accessories. Our journey began long before we set foot on the trail, as every step of preparation brought us closer to the pilgrimage of a lifetime. All our Camino stuff went with us on our 14-day vacation in Southern Spain prior to our pilgrimage.

Working with Caminoways, a Dublin-based travel agency specializing in Camino trips, Lorraine crafted the O'Grady Camino, a 6-day walking route from Sarria to Santiago de Compostela. She adjusted our flights home to extend our vacation and to accommodate the journey.

Our route allowed us to choose nightly accommodations, rather than relying on albergues (hostels for pilgrims that offer affordable short-term lodging with shared facilities). Pilgrims had to rise before dawn to secure a bed, as reservations were not accepted. It was first come, first served, verified by showing a pilgrim passport.

However, Caminoways' policy of one suitcase per hotel, limited to 20 kg (44 pounds), posed a challenge. Transitioning from a two-week vacation with heavier luggage made it difficult. My backpack was burdensome and unsuitable for a 6-day trek. Unlike traditional pilgrims who carried just two sets of clothes—one to wear and one to wash and dry—we needed gear.

We solved the luggage problem by leaving one suitcase and vacation items at our final destination, the Santiago de Compostela Parador. At the end of our vacation in Madrid, we flew into the Santiago de Compostela Airport, dropped off one set of luggage at the Parador, and were then driven to Sarria to begin our Camino.

The map below shows Galicia, Northwest Spain. The O'Grady Camino de Santiago (The French Way) started from Sarria with six nights of travel to Santiago De Compostela. Our destination towns after Sarria included Portomarin, Palas del Rel, Melinda, and Arzua and Santiago de Compostela (see map).

We quickly acquired our pilgrims passports which cost two

euros each and received our first stamp. The Camino Passport (Credencial del Peregrino) serves as evidence of having walked the 100 km to qualify for the Compostela or Certificate, the official documents that are testament to your journey.

Starting the Camino in Galicia, as we did from Sarria, Spain requires two stamps per day from churches, town halls, or other official establishments along the route to Santiago. Presenting your stamped pilgrims passport at the pilgrims' office enables you to apply for your Compostela certificate. Below is Lorraine's Camino de Santiago Passport adorned with stamps acquired during our journey from Sarria to Santiago de Compostela. The picture of Lorraine and me was taken at an exhibit just outside our hotel in Santiago; it was not part of the passport.

Before starting our Camino journey, we wandered around Sarria, exchanging greetings with fellow pilgrims. With the help of some Irish gentlemen, also Camino travelers, we found our nearby hotel. Later, during dinner, we met more Irish pilgrims, which fostered a sense of camaraderie.

## PORTOMARIN

On our first day from Sarria to Portomarin, we faced a 23 km (14+ miles) journey, which was estimated to take around six hours. Fully equipped with our rain gear, including my Green Bay Packer's rain parka with hood and pants, and Lorraine similarly suited up, we set out after breakfast. Despite the weather, we were mentally and physically prepared for the journey ahead.

Armed with our GPS and Caminoways maps detailing suggested stops and elevations, we set out expecting a serene walk-through villages and countryside paths. However, we were unprepared for how these country paths transformed into streams when it rained. About one hour into our journey, Lorraine remarked, "You know what this rain, mud, and cow smell remind me of?" I answered "Ireland." It bought back memories from our trip to Ireland in June 1981, where it rained every single day, even in the dry season.

We stopped at the Romanesque Church of Santiago de Barbadoro to get our passports stamped, ensuring we had at least two stamps, often three, per day. Afterward, we had lunch at Memoimentos and used the restroom—the last café and toilet until Portomarin.

In the restroom, I checked my hydration levels, realizing I was soaked, not from the rain but due to my non-breathable rain gear. I stripped down and opted to wear just my underwear beneath my rain gear. Pilgrims on longer stretches of the Camino discreetly managed their waste with a small shovel. If nature called, one simply wandered into the woods and dug a hole to relieve oneself.

As we neared the end of our first day's journey, we encountered two official signposts just before Portomarin: one indicating the Camino de Santiago straight ahead, and the other marked 'COMPLEMENTARIO.' With no clear view on either path, we approached three middle-aged gentlemen nearby for guidance. Despite the language barrier, one of them used hand gestures and drew lines in the dirt to indicate that the Camino de Santiago path, part of the ancient route, was the shorter option.

Following their suggestion, we continued along the Camino de Santiago path, only to encounter a very steep rock ravine with flowing water (see picture next page). We got punked!

We cautiously began our descent down the rocky path by moving slowly and using our hands for balance. Once we started, turning back was not an option; it was too slippery to climb back up. Our walking sticks proved useless, so we strapped them to our backpacks. It was a tense and slow journey, just a few inches each time. It took nearly forty minutes to reach the bottom of the ravine and step out of the water. Exhausted yet relieved, we took a moment to gather ourselves before pressing on toward Portomarin.

At a bus station along a main road into town, we encountered two of the guys who had given us route advice. Exhausted and still far from town, I chose to say nothing and simply walked by. We faced a daunting staircase straight up to reach our hotel, but after showering and changing, we managed to prepare for dinner. Having trekked nearly seven and a half hours in the rain that day, we were exhausted. At dinner, we observed other pilgrims, including my Irish friends, who looked refreshed—they had been relaxing at the hotel since early afternoon. It became clear that most pilgrims took the longer Complementario route, and after discussing with Caminoways, we confirmed that we had indeed been misled.

The next day presented another journey of 23 km. Clouds and rain blocked the sun, which prevented us from seeing our shadows as we headed eastward. We braced ourselves for a tough day, with the first half of the route comprising a challenging climb.

PALAS DE RE

We crossed the National Road LU-633 before proceeding along the pilgrim dirt road. Along the way, we passed by a landmark known as the 'chicken feed farm' which required us to cross the road again. As we encountered fellow pilgrims who passed by, we exchanged greetings of 'Buen Camino'. Some walked alongside us for a while, engaging in conversation about our starting point and origins.

Lorraine adjusted her pace to accommodate mine, ensuring we progressed together as we serpentined our way to the top.

We refrained from drinking from the fountains along the Camino and opted for soda instead, despite carrying sufficient water. At Ventas de Naron, we paused to get our passports stamped before embarking on the last 3km of our route which traversed a dirt path through woodland.

As we pressed on, we continually consulted our Caminoways walking maps and GPS. However, I could not shake the worry that we might have missed a crucial sign. I knew there was nothing behind us, so we kept walking. Relief washed over us when we finally spotted the Complejo de Cabana, our intended destination. Its wooden architecture evoked memories of a hotel in New York's Catskill Mountains. Stepping inside, we were greeted by the sight of our Irish companions enjoying a few cocktails.

After exchanging greetings, we inquired about their day. To our surprise, they had encountered no difficulties on route and easily found the parador. As we made our way to our rooms, I passed by a washer and dryer, knowing they would be my first stop after unpacking. Our clothes from the previous day were still damp, and my sneakers remained stubbornly wet. We quickly ran a wash-and-dry cycle before heading off for dinner. I had a chance to talk to our Irish friends who were about our age but managed to seem so fresh despite the journey. They laughed and revealed their secret: walking just enough in the morning to get two pilgrim stamps, then catching a cab to their next hotel after lunch.

The first two days of our Camino journey left me utterly exhausted. We trudged through rain-soaked paths, wading through mud and descending down a steep ravine. My backpack, laden with too much weight, pressed heavily on my shoulders. Despite the temptation to lighten my load, the challenging terrain and dimly lit woods compelled me to soldier on with everything I packed. The relentless exercise, coupled with the constant movement and perspiration, seemed to shed pounds from body with each step.

## MELIDE

Lorraine's meticulous planning made our third day on the Camino much more manageable, with a shorter 5 km (9 miles) journey to Melide. Melide is the only town where two Camino routes converge: the Camino Primitivo (Original Way) stops in Melinde, and the Camino Frances (French Way) passes through. Our Camino follows the French Way starting in Sarria.

We found ourselves walking alongside two former military individuals who opted to walk in sandals. Both started their journey in France and were aiming to cover the 500 miles to Santiago de Compostela. When I inquired about their choice of footwear, one explained that sandals allowed for quick drying of wool socks and prevented moisture retention and odor. Both individuals completed their U.S. service commitments and were undecided about their future. Independently, they discovered the Camino de Santiago and decided to embark on this journey, utilizing a combination of albergues (no reservations) along the way. One of the individuals missed a turn and struggled to find available lodging when he got back on track. Resorting to using his cell phone light as a guide, he continued walking through the night until he stumbled upon an albergue at sunrise. After having lunch together, we parted ways as we continued on our respective journeys.

Near the end of our journey, we sought out the roadside cross, 'cruceiro', which stands outside the San Roque Church, and is the oldest in Galicia. Each of us brought a rock from California with our names printed on it. As we placed these rocks on the cross, we said a prayer and symbolically released the 'upsets' that we left behind us on our way to Santiago de Compostela, seeking complete forgiveness of sins.

Just before reaching Arzua, we encountered a stand selling boiled octopus, a Galician delicacy. Despite being inland, Melinde is renowned for its best dish, *'Pulpo á Feira'* (boiled octopus), which is must-try. The vendor at the stand would cut off tentacles to order. However, some pilgrims likened the taste of octopus to the eraser on pencils, so we passed on the octopus experience.

Our journey stretched to nearly five hours, longer than anticipated, as we veered off the trail for sightseeing and encountered delays, such as waiting for a herd of sheep to pass by while we had lunch at a café. Taxis lined up and waited for the sheep to clear, including one for a woman with a bad ankle problem who needed to see a doctor. Some groups took advantage of the delay to embark on side trips, while some had already obtained their two passport stamps for the day and were headed for their next lodging. I did not spot my Irish friends during this time; our Camino spanned six days, whereas theirs was planned for five, ensuring our paths would not cross again.

Along the way, particularly through farmland, (most of our trip was through farmland) we often paused to let cows or sheep pass as they had the right of way. These animals were accustomed to pilgrims and paid little heed to their presence.

## AMENAL

We retired early to prepare for the upcoming 23km trek to Amenal. The route led through woodland, with a notable Y-junction at a Preguntono along a country road that you could not miss. Consulting our GPS and our Camino Walking Notes diligently, we ascended the steep uphill road to the right, passing beneath route N-547. Soon we found ourselves traversing a gravel track through crop fields, initially alone until two women caught up with us. Engaging in conversation, they realized they missed their turn to O Pino approximately 4km before Amenal. They deliberated whether to backtrack to their reserved hotel or join us and take a chance on getting a place to sleep in Amenal. Concerned by tales of pilgrims finding towns fully booked, they ultimately opted to return.

As we journeyed toward the town of Rua, we walked through a Eucalyptus forest and encountered stone farmhouses and traffic jams of cattle. While waiting, I hung my sneakers on a tree, a common sight as we approached the finals stage of our Camino. Our last night's stay in Amenal marked the end of our journey. Our last day to Santiago was another long walk, but we were really pleased with our effort so far, spreading our Camino walk out over six days. Lorraine's ankle was sore and got red and blue under the skin likely from navigating slippery surfaces. She wrapped her ankle with an ACE bandage and took extra strength Tylenol. She was good to go, and we headed off to Santiago.

We paused at Lavacolla, known as 'The Pilgrims Washing Place', where pilgrims traditionally cleansed themselves in the river before arriving in Santiago. Some pilgrim friends mentioned that 'lavar' means wash and 'ceullo' means neck in Spanish, indicating to 'wash the neck'. Rows of tall eucalyptus trees guided us to Monte de Gozo, or 'Mount Joy'. Here, we caught our first glimpse of the Cathedral of Santiago (below), illuminated by the sun.

We received our final passport stamp to meet the requirement of two stamps per day. Following the Camino km countdown signs to Santiago filled us with a sense of accomplishment. Despite Lorraine's foot pain, we felt elated. She smiled through the pain, and it was heartening to share this experience. Walking the last few miles was a joyous experience, especially as we were joined by many other pilgrims. Before reaching the center, we stopped for lunch to ensure we got a seat. Afterward, we checked in at the Parador, removed our backpacks, and confirmed that our luggage that traveled with us for our trip arrived before us via Caminoways. Everything was sorted out, a satisfying conclusion to our journey.

Afterward, we queued at the Pilgrims Office for an hour and a half to receive our Compostelas, the official certificates provided by the church to pilgrims who walked at least 100 km or cycled (or traveled by horse) 200 km to Santiago de Compostela. For pilgrims getting their Compostela meant they had secured a VIP ticket to heaven: "the 'Compostela' was considered an important paper, one to show St. Peter at the gates of heaven!" (Source: Caminoways).

The picture below is Lorraine's:

### The Camino Compostela

### CAMINO CERTIFICATE OF WELCOME

Pilgrims traveling for sport or cultural reasons can obtain a non-religious version of the Compostela, called the 'Certificate of Welcome'. The same rule of 100 km for walkers and 200 km for cyclists and horse riders applies for this certificate. We both received our Compostela and Certificate of Welcome. Source: Caminoways.

My Certificate of Welcome is shown below:

Walking through the Holy Door of Santiago Cathedral was a profound experience. Inside, guides directed us to the main altar in the cathedral and the crypt where the remains of Saint James the apostle are kept. After saying a prayer and exploring the church, we returned to the Holly Door. As we started to walk up to the Holy Door, one of the guides redirected us. In jest, I asked if our sins returned if we went back through the door, to which he just smiled and pointed us back into the church and the regular church doors.

As we stepped back into our Parador hotel, we were greeted by Margarete, our tour guide from 2015 who embraced us with joyful hugs. To her tour group, she shared the concept of a 'Camino Miracle', recounting how pilgrims often experience remarkable moments on their journey. Unaware that she had inspired our return to Spain and our Camino adventure, Margarete, truly embodied our own Camino miracle.

As we prepared to depart the next day, we ensured that our suitcases met the 50-pound limit for our flights home that evening. I signed us up for the rooftop tour of the Santiago Cathedral. Pilgrims had spoken of the breathtaking views from the cathedral roof, overlooking the plaza and the town. The ascent involved navigating a narrow stairway, with our guide pausing along the way to allow us to catch our breath. The climb was straight up but seemed endless, and my nerves grew as we ascended. I stopped counting at one hundred steps. Once on the roof, the views were indeed remarkable, but my anxiety overshadowed the experience. The rain made the tile surface slippery and with no railings, I felt uneasy. We returned just in time to get good seats for the 7:30 p.m. mass, grateful to have safely descended.

At mass, I made sure we secured seats close to the front because I wanted to film the botafumeiro swing. The botafumeiro, which means 'censer' in Galician, is a large liturgical vessel that hangs from the cathedral's dome and spreads incense throughout the temple as it swings from side to side, propelled by a system of pulleys.

The botafumeiro is operated by eight 'tiraboleiros', who are in charge of pushing it first and pulling the rope afterward, to make the container full of incense and coal pick up speed. The tiraboleiros can move the botafumeiro so that it reaches up to 68km/hour (42.25 miles/hour), going at a height of 21 meters (69 feet), drawing an arch of 65 meters (213 feet) (from website: Vive El Camino All about the Botafumeiro). I used my cell phone to film the flight of the botafumeiro. During this, an old nun with a beautiful voice sang from a lectern. The video with the sound remains one of our favorite mementos. YouTube has several videos of the Botafumeiro in the Cathedral of Santiago de Compostela.

We met nice people from all over the world on this journey. Each one was walking for a reason just as we were.

## 25

## ROWAM: BUILDING A BUSINESS

In May 2015, ROW expanded its footprint again in NYC and brought on board Phil Simotas as Senior Partner, COO, and Head of Business Development. Phil, previously President of FX Concepts, once oversaw Ryan, Jeff, Debra, Laurie, and Saurabh. With Phil's arrival, the ROW NYC office now sported a familiar FX Concepts vibe, catching the eye of visiting prospects.

I knew Phil from our time at FX Concepts from 2009 to 2011, during which the firm's AUM dropped significantly. I was surprised to see him join ROW, but I understood the need for administrative support in their NYC office. With tasks like reassessing U.S. mutual funds, expanding European capital introductions, and representing ROW at conferences, management thought Phil could take this role.

In 2015, I successfully secured approval for the ROW Diversified Fund, LP as an investment option for my IRA, and Roth IRA accounts through the Schwab Alternative Investment Group. This involved extensive collaboration with ROW's Laurie Pisano and the Schwab team. Fast forward to June 2019, I worked with Laurie Pisano and Monica Napoli to facilitate the approval of two new

ROW programs, ROW Diversified 2X Fund, LP and the ROW RV Fund, LP, with the Schwab AI Committee. I invested in all three ROW programs through Schwab.

A major pension consultant firm explored expanding ROW's Diversified program and considered adding a 2X version. Though I never directly interacted with the senior investment research consultant, I worked with two talented staff individuals for two years to arrange a meeting with their boss and Ryan at the 2015 Context Summit Conference. Subsequently, they worked with Ryan to develop the relationship further and finalize the deal on ROW Diversified 2X Fund.

On May 17, 2017, the Institutional Investor's Alpha ranked hedge funds based on their fundraising abilities. ROW Asset Management secured the impressive #3 spot out of 100. I had not seen this Hedge Fund Marketing Power Index before and decided to research. Phil recently updated the ROW Diversified marketing book and perhaps that played a role in our ranking.

The years 2015 and 2016, which Alpha selected, were significant for ROW Asset Management, as we experienced considerable growth in Asset Under Management (AUM). This surge was primarily fueled by the robust performance of the ROW Diversified strategy. Investors showed increased interest after witnessing the strategy's resilience during the May/June 2013 drawdown and its impressive results in 2014, boasting a net return of 27.11%.

Additionally, the introduction of the ROW Diversified 2X Fund program in 2016 played a pivotal role in growth trajectory. This program offered investors an enhanced investment opportunity. Receiving recognition from everyone for all the hard work was rewarding.

When Morgan Stanley replaced Société Générale as a trading partner for ROW Asset Management, I lost my marketing contacts at Newedge Société Générale. However, ROW established a new partnership with Goldman Sachs, and Bob Puccio, VP at Goldman

Sachs, became our marketing contact. Since Phil had prior experience with Bob, I ensured close coordination by contacting Phil first and always copying him on emails to Bob.

Phil diligently followed up on prospects from the 2015 Florida Summit conference, spending a year familiarizing a Midwest prospect with ROW offerings. Ryan then engaged in multiple conversations to solidify the relationship. In January 2016, the prospect invested in our ROW Diversified Fund, as a result of which it surpassed $100 million for the first time. Today the ROW Diversified Fund is $1.2 billion.

Ryan spoke at Goldman Sachs' annual alternative investment conference in London every October to discuss ROW Diversified, our models, and risk systems. Just as I did with Mike Boss, I regularly updated our contact lists with Goldman and Morgan Stanley, incorporating new names from each firm. Maintaining our extensive contact list was essential, given the significant turnover in the hedge fund industry.

From 2016 to 2018, my days were filled with research, calls, emails, and repetition. Dealing with bounced emails and 'unknown sender' notifications made it tougher. To cope, I often pretended to be a character from radio or TV. For instance, if it was a prospect from Yale, I might leave a message hinting that we might have met at Rudy's bar on Elm Street in New Haven.

In 2019, at the MFA June meeting, I aimed to secure a Chicago-area pension investment for ROW. Despite a canceled meeting with a prospect, a connection with their pension consultant, who had prior experience with ROW, led to discussions with Ryan about a potential investment. Ultimately, ROW competed with FORT for the assignment, and Ryan secured the deal.

Over nine years at ROW, I faced the challenge of convincing prospects to meet with our small but successful CTA. My determination was fueled by a deeper motivation: my son. Despite obstacles, I persisted, driven by stubbornness and a belief in ROW's potential. Collaborating with a small team of intelligent individuals united by a common goal was a unique experience. Together, we built a first-class systematic program tailored for the future.

Since the 1970s, the investment landscape has undergone a remarkable transformation, with alternative investments now comprising a substantial portion of global assets. As reported by Barron's, pension assets surpassed $56 trillion in 2023, with alternative assets accounting for over 20% of this total. Today, prospects inquire why they should choose ROW over other options rather than questioning the relevance of ROW altogether.

## 26

## THE NEXT STEP

Facing a health scare like prostate cancer forces you to reevaluate your priorities. Retirement seemed distant until my Prostate Specific Antigen (PSA) levels spiked unexpectedly. The biopsy revealed an aggressive form of cancer that required urgent treatment. I chose Stereotactic Body Radiotherapy (SBRT) at UCLA, Westwood, CA, for its precise targeting of intense radiation on the affected area because it offered a promising alternative to traditional surgery. So far, so good!

Retirement was not on the horizon, so I had not considered pursuing hobbies or pastimes for my golden years. However, facing this health challenge prompted me to reevaluate my priorities and explore new interests.

The writing course marked a turning point for me. Reflecting on my career in the ever-evolving investment world felt like the right choice. I witnessed firsthand the shifts and changes that shaped the industry. Incorporating O'Grady genealogy, which had led me to become an Irish citizen, added an intriguing layer to my narrative and intertwined it with my business journey.

Digging into genealogy sparked a profound interest in history for me. Exploring ancestry websites to trace both my maternal and paternal family lines, I became captivated by the stories and connections to be unearthed. A significant discovery emerged: an Irish family history intertwined with my own. With much work ahead, I am excited to delve deeper into this journey each day.

# APPENDIX

CHAPTER 1

### Thanksgiving—California

Thanksgiving November 1995, with Tiger Sharks vs. Blackhawks playing hockey wearing roller blades. Pictures 1 and 2 below are my four sons Ryan, Christopher, James, goaltender Mark, my two nieces Lauren and Kristen, and goal tender Jin Park O'Grady, Ryan's wife.

Thanksgiving November 1996, basketball on the same court. The score was different in 1996 because Maureen could really shoot.

## CHAPTER 2

### Ownership—Green Bay Packers

### Federal Reserve Chairman G. William Miller

On October 18, 1984, I attended a conference at Fairfield University where former Federal Reserve Chairman G. William Miller was speaking. I introduced myself to G. William Miller afterward, and he kindly signed my program with a message. However, he did not remember mom.

## CHAPTER 9

John F. Eckstein, whom I encountered once at the Colonial Bank Board Meeting with Miles Slater is mentioned in Roger Lowenstein's book *When Genius Failed-The Rise and Fall of Long-Term Capita*l. In June 1979, Eckstein found himself in a challenging arbitrage position with U.S. Treasury Bills. Seeking assistance, he approached Salomon Brothers, where rising star John Meriwether convinced Salomon to buy out Eckstein. Despite initial difficulties, prices eventually converged, resulting in a profitable outcome for Salomon. The incident market the beginning of Meriwether's rise that led to the establishment of Long-Term Capital, a legendary hedge fund based in Greenwich, Connecticut.

Miles Slater becomes CEO of Salomon Brothers International.

## CHAPTER 13

**Weston Maintenance sweatshirt**

**President Kiwanis Club 1993–1994**

# THE EXCEPTIONAL LIFE OF AN ORDINARY MAN

## Currency Risk in Investment Portfolios Paperback — June 1, 1999

## Developing a Currency Hedge Ratio:
## Timothy J. O'Grady, Janice B. Naarden and Steven E. Peplowski

VOLUME 2, NUMBER 2        FALL 1997

# JOURNAL of PENSION PLAN INVESTING

Editor: Joelyn Flomenhaft

- ISSUES CONCERNING CAPITALIZATION-
  WEIGHTED BENCHMARKS IN
  EMERGING MARKETS
  *Jon Lukomnik*
- A CASE FOR DISTRESSED SECURITIES
  INVESTING
  *Wilbur L. Ross, Jr.*
- CONSIDERATIONS IN THE DESIGN
  OF INVESTMENT OPTIONS FOR
  DEFINED CONTRIBUTION PLANS
  *Robin S. Pellish and
  Anne C. Buehl*
- THE GROWTH OF INSTITUTIONAL
  INVESTMENT IN REITs
  *Jay L. Willoughby*
- CUSTODY BANKING: A
  RETIREMENT SYSTEM GUIDE TO
  SELECTION OPTIMIZATION
  *Paul Matson and LeRoy Gilbertson*
- DEVELOPING A CURRENCY HEDGE
  RATIO
  *Timothy J. O'Grady,
  Janice B. Naarden and
  Steven E. Peplowski*

GUEST COLUMNS
EXAMINING THE OPTIONS OF
CONVERTING TO A DEFINED
CONTRIBUTION RETIREMENT PLAN
FROM A DEFINED BENEFIT PLAN IN
THE STATE OF VERMONT
*James H. Douglas*
HONG KONG AFTER 1997:
IMPLICATIONS FOR U.S. PENSION
PLAN SPONSORS
*Sarah H. Kesserer*

- PUBLICATION POLICIES FOR AUTHORS

A PANEL
PUBLICATION
*Aspen Publishers, Inc.*

## CHAPTER 18

## Hollywood Walk of Fame Plaques

CHAPTER 21

**FX Concepts**
**Nine currencies programmed for GRA**

- **AUD:** Australian Dollar
- **CAD:** Canadian Dollar- G7 Currency
- **EUR:** Euro-European Union-G7 currency
- **GBP:** British Pound-G7 currency
- **JPY:** Japanese Yen-G7 currency
- **NOK:** Norwegian Krone
- **NZD:** New Zealand Dollar
- **SEK:** Swedish Krona
- **USD:** U.S. Dollar-G7 currency

# ABOUT THE AUTHOR

In reflecting on my journey, I realize how fortunate I've been to have support during pivotal moments in my life. Lorraine, my wife through thick and thin, has been my rock, guiding me through difficult decisions and celebrating triumphs alongside me.

Family has always been a cornerstone of my life. With four sons and seven grandchildren, I feel immensely blessed. While my two oldest sons, Ryan and James, chose to follow me into the investment world, their paths were their own—though I often jokingly take credit for all of it. Mark heads an IT division of a Fortune 500 global company in Connecticut, and Christopher is a controller, set up his own LLC to a series of offshore companies.

The decision to uproot from Connecticut at the age of fifty-four was one of the toughest I've faced. Saying goodbye to my mother, my brother Tom and his family, my close college friends was not easy. However, with three of our sons eventually joining us in California, the move took on a new vibrancy, even amidst the challenges.

Change, I've come to learn, is never easy, especially when you are the lone advocate for a new idea. But it's in those moments of uncertainty and solitude that I've often found my greatest strength and resilience.

Thank you for taking the time to read my memoir. If you enjoyed it, please consider leaving a review on Amazon, Goodreads, or your favorite website.

# ACKNOWLEDGMENTS

In expressing gratitude, I want to extend my deepest appreciation to those who have been instrumental in shaping my journey.

First, I must thank my family for their unwavering support and understanding, allowing me the time and space to reflect on my experiences and write my memoir. And for not making fun of me typing with just two fingers.

Thank you to Michael Sheeler, whose willingness to review my manuscript multiple times and assist with refining images of pictures of my parents and grandparents.

To Ben Hoffman of Colonial Bank, I extend my sincerest thanks for affording me the opportunity to develop the Trust Trading role—a pivotal starting point in my career. Joseph Carlson II's guidance during my thirteen-year tenure with Colonial's Treasury/Investment Department was invaluable, and I am grateful for his mentorship.

Nancy Pierpoint and Mark Hansen deserve special mention for their unwavering support in nurturing our Investment Group and Municipal Bond Department.

I am deeply grateful to Joseph Michael McManus for his friendship and professional guidance during my early days as Colonial Bank portfolio manager. Thanks for introducing me to Miles Slater who helped me at Colonial, and Roosevelt & Cross and Halbert Lindquist with whom I worked at Western Asset.

I thank Don McDonald of Roosevelt & Cross for his collaborative efforts in building our fixed-income business.

To Tony Minopoli, Mike Randazzo, Janice Naarden, John Cardinali, and Alec Rapaport of EAI I owe a debt of gratitude for their unwavering support and camaraderie as we built the best Fixed Income and Currency Research Group at Evaluation Associates Inc. Alec, in particular, continued to champion my efforts even during my tenure at Western Asset.

Chad Monroe's immediate engagement with fixed income work accelerated my career trajectory, and I am immensely grateful for his contributions. The consulting team at Colonial Bank, including Chad, Bill Brock, Ellen Petrino, Jeanne Gustafson, Linda Schlissel, John Gardner, and my friend Larry Zielinski, left an indelible impression on me with their unmatched experience and creativity. It was a pleasure and an honor to collaborate with each of you.

Steve Saruwatari of Western Asset deserves special mention for his assistance in building our Product Development Group. I am grateful to Kevin Ehrlich of Western Asset's legal team and Brian Chegwidden, Partner of Ropes & Gray for their legal support in launching my projects.

Jay Choi and Al McClymonds of Western Asset played pivotal roles in building a first-class relative value fixed income hedge fund, SGOF and I am grateful for their dedication.

David Lerman of the Chicago Mercantile Exchange (CME) deserves recognition for his assistance with Western's Portable Alpha products and my efforts at ROW Asset Management.

My heartfelt thanks to investment managers Fred Horton, Mark Kritzman, Dan Fuss, Phil Nehro, Olaf Rogge, Mark Turner, Rory MacLeod, Adrian Lee, Ron Layard Liesching, Tom Kendall, Halbert Linquist, and Mike Lamont for helping me understand fixed income and currency strategies and processes.

A special shout-out to John Flint of Credit Suisse for his unwavering support and for opening numerous doors throughout my career journey.

Each of these individuals has played a role in shaping my journey and for that I am eternally grateful.

www.ingramcontent.com/pod-product-compliance
Lightning Source LLC
Chambersburg PA
CBHW020635220526
45464CB00001B/159